The book was easy to follow an⌖⌖⌖⌖⌖⌖⌖⌖⌖⌖⌖⌖ ⌐ı⌐e to engage
with the workbook-type format ⌐⌐⌐⌐⌐⌐ ⌐ıe steps to create a
name for my business. There are maıy little tips and techniques that,
honestly, most of us never think about. Interestingly though, once
you learn them, you'll have a better idea of why some iconic brands
have such great names. A perfect book for those considering new
business ventures or rebranding with a name change.

—DAVE SEVIGNY, SERIAL ENTREPRENEUR AND
FOUNDER OF VOLTA TECHNOLOGY

We've partnered with Brad and his team to name several
products. A good name is critical at every stage, from getting early
traction to scaling a business. Brad was incredible at coming up
with a wide array of candidates and then thinking through
the journey of each option.

—ANDREW BOROVSKY, HEAD OF PRODUCT, CADRE

My favorite part of the process was that the team first took the
time to understand our company culture and values. From there,
we received distinct concepts that were diverse and aligned with
different aspects of our culture. The end result was natural,
authentic, and memorable. It inspired our employees.

—TAYLOR AMERMAN, GLOBAL ALCOHOL RESPONSIBILITY MANAGER,
BROWN-FORMAN

I used *The Naming Book* to help me name my new business. I was a complete newbie and had no idea where to start. I worked through the exercises in the book with the help of friends and family. One night when we were putting different words together as instructed by the book, we came upon the perfect name. Every time I started to feel overwhelmed and frustrated by the process, I went back and did another exercise until I landed on the right name. Having the steps clearly laid out made the process so much easier.

—HELEN NONN, ENTREPRENEUR, WOVEN WONDER

As my clients start the branding process with me, they often realize that in addition to a new visual identity, the company's name needs to be updated. Guiding them through these naming exercises helps me develop a new brand that is more accurate and reflective of the company's mission and personality.

—STEVIE MORRSON, ENTREPRENEUR AND GRAPHIC DESIGNER

THE NAMING BOOK

↓ ↓ ↓

5 steps to creating brand and product names that sell

BRAD FLOWERS

Entrepreneur Press®

Entrepreneur Press, Publisher
Cover Design: Andrew Welyczko
Production and Composition: Eliot House Productions

This publication is designed to provide accurate and authoritative information in regard
to the subject matter covered. It is sold with the understanding that the publisher is not
engaged in rendering legal, accounting, or other professional services. If legal advice
or other expert assistance is required, the services of a competent professional person
should be sought.

Entrepreneur Press® is a registered trademark of Entrepreneur Media, Inc.

Library of Congress Cataloging-in-Publication Data
    Names: Flowers, Brad, author.
    Title: The naming book : five steps to creating brand and product names that sell / by
        Brad Flowers.
    Description: Irvine, California : Entrepreneur Media, Inc., 2020. | Summary: "A name can
        be a business's first impression, a product's calling card, and a brand's defining
        characteristic, and choosing a name out of thin air could cause devastating results.
        In The Naming Book, Brad Flowers, partner at branding agency Bullhorn Creative,
        presents a clear and actionable five-step framework to naming anything"-- Provided
        by publisher.
    Identifiers: LCCN 2019049276 (print) | LCCN 2019049277 (ebook) | ISBN 978-1-
        59918-666-5 (paperback) | ISBN 978-1-61308-423-6 (ebook)
    Subjects: LCSH: Brand name products. | Business names. | Branding (Marketing)
    Classification: LCC HD69.B7 F585 2020 (print) | LCC HD69.B7 (ebook) | DDC--
        dc8.8/27 23 65
    LC record available at https://lccn.loc.gov/2019049276
    LC ebook record available at https://lccn.loc.gov/2019049277

Printed in the United States of America

24 23 22 21 20   10 9 8 7 6 5 4 3 2 1

Choosing a name is like driving a racing car.
To win, you have to take chances!

—Al Ries and Jack Trout,
Positioning: The Battle for Your Mind

CONTENTS

INTRODUCTION

George Vancouver spent nearly as much of his life on the water as on land. He was born in the middle of the eighteenth century, at the height of European exploration, in a port town north of London. At the age of 13, he volunteered for the Royal Navy and went to sea.

He was taken on as an apprentice by Captain James Cook and was onboard for the mapping of the east coast of Australia and the circumnavigation of New Zealand, a voyage that lasted three years. During the same timespan when I went from starting puberty to my first school dance to driving a car, he hardly set foot off the boat. He liked it enough to do it again right away. This time, he was gone for four years. At his age, I was playing high school baseball, graduating, and going off to college. Vancouver was still on a boat.

His dedication paid off, though. Before the age of 40, he was made a captain of the Royal Navy and tasked with finding the Northwest Passage, a long-sought-after route connecting the Pacific and Atlantic Oceans by sailing through the Canadian Arctic. If he could find it, the results would be lucrative for British trade. Since he was going the long way around anyway, he started off exploring the Pacific islands. He then went on to San Francisco and proceeded north.

In addition to exploring, he was also tasked with creating maps of the Pacific coast. He eventually concluded that there was no Northwest Passage, but he did make some valuable discoveries. He also left his mark on the geography of the Pacific Northwest. The most notable part of the expedition was the mapping of the Inside Passage from Seattle to Alaska. In fact, creating these maps became a big part of Vancouver's legacy.

Captain Vancouver was a well-trained cartographer. He could certainly manage his ship and crew. He was not, however, prepared for all the naming he was about to do. At that time, mapping meant he would need new names for the places he encountered on his journey. He likely didn't have the criteria to decide if a name was good. He didn't have any tools to generate ideas. And his research tools onboard were severely limited.

Once they moved into the Inside Passage, the captain and his crew discovered a large island, and (no surprises here) he named it Vancouver Island. His names didn't get much more creative than that, unfortunately, even though they persist more than 200 years later. What could have been a master class in memorable naming reads more like a laundry list.

He sprinkled in some benefactors and a few significant naval names, and then quickly ran out of steam. Eddies, whirlpools, inlets, and straits were a roll call of everyone and anything he had ever known. In his classic book, *Vancouver's Discovery of Puget Sound*, Edmond Meany identifies these examples of Captain Vancouver's lackluster naming conventions[1]:

+ Puget Sound. Named after his lieutenant, Peter Puget.
+ Port Gardner. Named after his colleague, Vice Admiral Sir Alan Gardner.
+ Port Susan. Named after Gardner's wife, Susanna.
+ Mount St. Helens. Named after his friend the Baron St. Helens.
+ Mount Rainier. Named after his colleague and friend Rear Admiral Peter Rainier.
+ Mount Baker. Named after the guy who first saw it, James Baker.
+ Whidbey Island. Named after explorer Joseph Whidbey.
+ Vashon Island. Named after a colleague, Captain James Vashon.

Given the amount of time Captain Vancouver spent on a boat in his life, these names aren't surprising. Of course he would name things after other explorers, his fellow sailors, and other people he knew. He pulled liberally from the names around him. The starkest example of this is the name of his ship, HMS *Discovery*. He didn't choose his ship's name, but he did name four different places after it. There is a Discovery Bay, Discovery Passage, Discovery Island, and Port Discovery.

The persistence of these names hints at the power of naming. To name something is to claim it. Renaming something is a way of staking ownership, of asserting dominance. The places Captain Vancouver encountered already had perfectly good names, given by the Native Americans who lived in the area, but he didn't bother to learn them—or, if he did, he chose not to use them. The names we ended up using lack cultural context, since we're unaware of the long history of the area before Vancouver arrived. Contrast the names from Vancouver with names that persist from the people indigenous to the region. There are place names such as Sammamish, Snohomish, and Seattle. There is the city, Yakima, that has also become a brand name for a leading manufacturer of car racks. These names sound and feel different. They have a different resonance with the places they represent. The people who live there are connected to history in a different way. Names are powerful, as is the thought process behind it, because names reverberate through time.

Captain Vancouver isn't unique in how he chose to name the places he discovered or reclaimed. The era of European exploration provides clear examples of naming conventions because so many things were renamed then, and we live with many of those names to this day. It shows us that without the proper tools to create names, we tend to do what everyone else is doing.

Sticking with the history theme, King George III was in power during the height of English colonial activity in North America. He was preceded by his grandfather, King George II. Some original thinker probably thought, "I am going to call this place Georgetown in honor of the king." It has a ring to it. Not all Georgetowns were named after the king. Some were named after the landowner, the previous landowner, a family member, or themselves. There are over 20 other Georgetowns in the United States, not to mention three in Australia, four in Canada (one of which is a ghost town), two in India, and one apiece in South Africa (now simplified to George), Malaysia, the Bahamas, Belize, and Guyana. That is a lot of Georgetowns.

I am not pointing fingers at those who aren't terribly original in their naming process. I have a son named George. There is something to be said for tradition. However, relying on it when coming up with a name can make it hard to stand out. I live in central Kentucky. There is a small liberal arts college nearby called Georgetown College. I was recently in a long conversation with a student talking about how they were attending Georgetown and had become interested in branding. It was 30 minutes before I realized they meant *the Georgetown*. After all, it isn't immediately clear which Georgetown you're referring to in conversation. And you will likely want whatever you are naming—most likely your company—to be immediately clear.

The way to create clarity is by using an intentional strategy— because, as we've shown, tradition isn't really a strategy. It is the path of least resistance. But that path isn't the best choice because your business will be fighting for your potential customers' attention. Your name is your first weapon in that battle. People will either read it and forget it or pause for a second and wonder, "What is this?" You only need your name to buy you that second. If you get that, your packaging design, website, or great product can do the rest.

If you want a name that sounds like all the other names in your industry, stop here. Don't waste your time. Name your island after yourself and call it a day.

This book teaches you how to establish a naming strategy and generate names that work. It also shows you how to establish the criteria you will use to judge the names you generate. Knowing how to evaluate your name may be your biggest challenge; it is hard to know what makes one name better than another. The water is murky and the decision can seem arbitrary. The process in this book takes you through five steps to determine what is important to you, create a matrix that is customized to your business, and give you the clarity you need to choose a name that will last.

ORIGIN STORY

I have to give you a little back story to make sense of how I came to run a branding company and write this book. I would like to say that I already had the expertise to name businesses when I started the company. It isn't true, though. I had to screw up a thousand times to get here.

When I started the business with a friend in 2008, we had no experience and no clients. Well, I had *some* experience—just not *relevant* experience. I moved furniture. I installed Christmas lights. I sold books. I waited tables and tended bar. I managed a bike shop. I worked a lot of jobs I didn't want to do anymore. But with each job change, I was slowly accumulating the criteria I needed to decide on my career. I knew I wanted a job where I could learn. I wanted to interact with people. I wanted to do something creative and meaningful, to have the sense that I was improving the world in some way. I was ambitious enough to want the opportunity to move upward. And it may sound stupid, but after standing on concrete floors at the bike shop for four years, I wanted a job where I could sit down.

I learned two other important things at that job selling bikes. First, I realized that I really love business. I love the simple act of selling something to someone: the challenge of predicting what they might want and the thrill of helping them find the perfect thing that could change their life. This was something of a surprise because I have a degree in literature. I had always assumed I would become a teacher. What else would someone who likes to read books do for a living? Then I took a job as a substitute teacher for a year. That was eye-opening. I found that while I love literature, I didn't really care for teaching. In particular, I didn't like teaching people who didn't have the same passion I did.

This background gave me an interesting perspective, but it hadn't prepared me for the nuts and bolts of business. I couldn't analyze a profit and loss (P&L) statement. I certainly didn't know what a balance sheet was. While I may have loved it, my real-world business experience was extremely limited.

Second, I realized marketing was an interesting challenge. At one point, the owner of the shop sent me to meet with a committee putting on a citywide bike event. I worked with the committee members to set the route, coordinate with the police for road closures, and promote the event. I found that I really liked promoting something I thought was important—in this case, that people should rediscover the joy of bike riding in their city.

That gets us back to 2008 and the day I quit my job at the bike shop. While I liked working with people, I wanted to work in a less retail-based environment where I could focus on interacting more deeply with fewer people. I also wanted more of an intellectual challenge.

But the world was in the middle of an economic downturn. No one was hiring. And I wasn't particularly qualified for the jobs I wanted. To find a job that met my criteria, I would have to create it, and I quickly realized I would need to start a business. I knew I wanted to help promote businesses, events, nonprofits, and anyone else who would pay us. The first challenge was what to call this new venture.

At the time, my house was under construction, so my partner and I were sitting at the laundromat. We had a pen and a blank sheet of paper and only a very general idea of what the business would do. The paper stayed blank for the whole wash cycle. By the time the clothes were in the dryer, we started getting some words down. We were thinking of things that gave comfort. Shade trees. Things we liked. Bicycles. Music. We were wondering why people would hire us: to be heard. Megaphone. Microphone. Bullhorn. That's it: Bullhorn!

It might have been the ideal match for our business, or it might have been sparked by the repetitive thump, thump, thump of the dryers. Either way, there was something to it. Maybe it was a little obvious, but it has turned out to be a workable name for what would become our branding agency.

Ten years later, Bullhorn has found its place in the world—at the intersection of what we are good at, what people will pay us to do, and what makes a positive impact on our community and the world. As our company changes, with smart people coming and going over the years, our focus changes, too. Today we build confident brands with language and design. And, yes, I like to think about the language part.

That's one reason naming businesses became part of our corporate identity. While we had never considered making "naming" a part of what we did (after all, it took us a few wash cycles to get our own name right), the opportunity landed on our doorstep.

Finding Our Niche

We had been in business a little less than two years when a nonprofit approached us with a problem. They wanted to pivot their organization to better accomplish their mission. Like many nonprofits, they had an unruly acronym for a name. They knew that name wouldn't work for their new venture, which was more public-facing, and asked us to help figure out a new one. It wasn't our usual line of work, but we weren't about to let a lack of expertise get in the way.

I loved words. I loved thinking about how people use words. But I had no process for coming up with a name. It was so much harder than I ever could have guessed. It was like walking in the darkness with little glints of light that disappear when you reach for them: ideas that seem perfect have already been taken by someone else or have an unanticipated negative connotation. At one point, I became attached to a name only to find out it was the name of a popular porn website. The client didn't think that was the image they were looking for. But that idea sparked the next one, which stuck.

Our client's organization was creating an incubator to grow young nonprofits. The first concept we came up with was "greenhouse." It's a great metaphor but probably too obvious. We then turned to "hothouse": a greenhouse that is heated. That metaphor is even better: They are providing the space and services that allow organic interactions to spur growth. However, *hothouse* unfortunately intersected in the SEO world with pornography. Don't look it up—you will regret it.

We still thought we were on the right track, though. We had a long list of words derived from organic and industrial terms. Two words stood out: *plant* and *factory*. I thought maybe the name could be Plant Factory, but it sounded too much like a big-box retailer. After staring at it for a long time, I started to play with it. First, I changed it to Plantfactory. That was too long, and I didn't like the *t* to *f* transition. Then I tried removing some letters. After getting rid of the first syllable of *factory*, I had Plantory. I didn't know enough then to set out my criteria. But if I had, I would have said it was unique, easy to say, sounded like a place, and included strong consonants. They liked it. The company became The Plantory. It is doing great work to this day.

We made it through that project bedraggled but intrigued. It was creative and chaotic. But I loved the bedlam: the lists of words all over the table, the thesaurus lying open, a real paper dictionary, an article about Pan the nature god. It was stressful, but fun. There was a point when I was sure we would never have a good idea, and then it came. It has been my experience again and again that if you stick it out, the good idea will eventually arrive.

We decided to narrow our focus from generalized marketing to a more targeted focus on branding. We were no longer just promoting things we liked. We wanted to help companies communicate better. To us, that started with clarifying their visual identity: logo, colors, photography, etc. It also meant evaluating the way they spoke about themselves.

Over time, more people came to us thinking they needed to evaluate their company name. Because of my educational background, I headed all the naming projects. To be clear, reading books doesn't necessarily prepare you to name companies, but being an avid reader with a literature degree certainly helps you interact with words and language.

As clients hired us more often to create names, I realized I needed help. I hired friends who thought about language in interesting ways: poets, songwriters, editors. They were excited about the job but frustrated by the process. I would give them a creative brief, but no clear road map. They could generate a lot of words, but they were never sure which ones would be chosen. I knew we needed more ideas to be good at our job, but I didn't have a systematic way to do that.

And that is the pain point that started this project.

WHAT YOU CAN NAME USING THIS BOOK

You might have the nagging thought that a step-by-step process for naming your business won't work for you. You may be concerned that you will spend time you don't have working on this and not get anything better than what you have now. You might think your situation is complicated or unique. And maybe it is. But often, something feels complicated just because you don't have the right tools or instructions.

This book has the tools and instructions you need to name your business. It is a process built through real-world experiences and informed by academic research (though I won't bore you with too much academic speak). It will help you face what seems like an impossible task one step at a time. If you put in the effort, you will end up with a great name.

I think this is important because businesses have a huge impact on the world. They provide jobs, opportunity, and a tax base, among other benefits. A good name is key to a successful business. This is one of your first steps toward creating that business.

This process isn't just for naming businesses, though. I use the word "business" or "company" throughout the book as general terms. But in my company, we have used this process to name buildings, nonprofits, associations, churches, schools, and cultural institutions. We have even named a few children. Within a company, it can be used to name products, services, divisions, and even business segments. So when you see the word "company," you can easily substitute "product," "nonprofit," or whatever else you're trying to name.

As the general public becomes more design savvy, and as the internet breaks down barriers to information, the differences between the groups above start to seem trivial. Businesses become more aware of their various stakeholders. Nonprofits establish business best practices. Churches and cities hire creative directors. Ultimately, just about anything can benefit from a more thoughtful name. I trust this process to work for you regardless of what you are naming. I am certain your organization will benefit from it. Your constituents deserve clarity, and that starts with a good name.

NAMING: PART OF THE JOURNEY

It may go without saying, but, yes, the name of a business is pretty important. It is the first big decision that makes other decisions easier. It sets the tone for what the logo should look like, for what colors make sense, and for the rest of the internal and external brand language (more on this later). A company called Apple is going to look and sound fundamentally different from a company called Microsoft.

Prepare yourself mentally for what is to come. The best name in the world will sound strange initially. As Robert Leduc notes in his book *How to Launch a New Product*, the name sounds strange because it is out of context. You will never again see just the name on a piece of paper. You will see the brand.

Over time, a name comes to represent the organization and lend cachet to its brand value.

However, your own experience with that organization can change how you perceive the name. For example, no name in the world will make you like your internet provider if their rates continue to go up, your service is intermittent, and you can't get anyone on the phone to help you. No matter how much you like the name "Ikea," if they short you hardware on one shipment and send something broken in the next, your feelings will change—and not for the better.

In other words, a name does not stand alone. It changes in relation to consumer interaction. One example is the Ford Edsel, a failure so dramatic that it is covered in business classes around the world. The name is often cited as a reason for the failure. It was named after Henry Ford's son, Edsel Ford. It is probably not a good name for a car, but that was only part of the problem. The marketing was a disaster. The car had reliability problems. The taillights were shaped like arrows, so when the turn signals were on they looked like they were pointing in the wrong direction. And many people simply thought it was an ugly car.

Did the Edsel fail because of marketing, design, or manufacturing? Or was it the name? Names are complicated because they live within the brand ecosystem; they are part of the "brand personality." In other words, the name is only part of the experience you have with a brand. You also experience a brand through their graphic design choices and how (or if) they answer the phone. You might interact with an employee the company hired and trained. You go to the company's physical location or their website. You actually use the product or service.

That's not to say the name isn't an important part of the brand strategy. Put simply, your brand strategy is your long-term plan for how your product or service will interact with the public. That strategy can include marketing, design, manufacturing, etc. The name is important because it becomes the shorthand for all those interactions in the consumer's mind.

The fact that there is more to an organization than the name can be liberating. Yes, choosing a name is difficult, but relax—the name is only part of the experience. A good name can give a good business an advantage, but the best name in the world can't save a bad business.

Think of your business like an iceberg. The name is the tip. The tip is important, because that's the part we see. The name really has to do two things. It has to distinguish your iceberg from similar ones, and it can't misrepresent the iceberg. Don't try to claim it's a volcano or a rainforest. The rest of the iceberg is your business model, employees, service, product, location, and culture. Just like with icebergs, there is much more going on with your business under the surface.

Names are important, but let's face it: Organizations with bad names succeed all the time. And companies with good names fail. That doesn't mean this process you are about to go through isn't important. It just means that it isn't the only important thing you have to do.

Remember, you don't have to strike oil with this name. By that, I mean you don't need to stress if the right name doesn't immediately appear. Naming a business is a journey, made up of stops along the way. You are on a road trip, and all you have to do is find one gas station, and then the next. Before you know it, you're there.

HOW TO USE THIS BOOK

I have taken the naming process we have developed at Bullhorn over the past ten years and organized it into five steps for you.

This process has proved successful across industries as diverse as nonprofit, finance, IT, online learning, and health care. It has worked for new and established businesses and for very different sorts of people.

I am a pragmatist. I like what works. This system is oriented toward three primary goals:

1. Understanding what your name needs to do
2. Generating the raw materials (words)
3. Using the words to make names

This isn't about what I like. This isn't (exclusively) about what makes for an aesthetically pleasing name—that may not matter for your organization. This system is about finding a name that gives you a competitive advantage. Is it important if you like it? Probably. Because liking your name will give you confidence, and that will give you a competitive advantage.

Here is a quick snapshot of the process. The following sections of the book will be organized around these steps:

Step 1: Establishing Criteria

Think of naming as a game where you get to make up the rules. You'd never know who wins if you didn't know the rules. In the same way, you won't know if you have a successful name until you know what makes a name good or bad. Of course, there are some general guidelines. This step helps you establish rules that make sense in your context.

Step 2: Brainstorming

Naming doesn't mean sitting around waiting for a name to magically appear in your brain. It is about generating lots of words, which often isn't a natural process for most people. We have two tricks to help you limber up and start rattling off words that might seem disjointed at first. First, we think of concrete images related to your business. Second, we get a little abstract. Don't worry—it will be fun.

Step 3: Compiling Names

In this step, we move from lists of words to shorter lists of names by introducing different types of names. You use your lists to populate these different types with potential names. Each type of name has its own exercise to help you think about words in new ways.

Step 4: Expanding Your Knowledge

The best name just might not be in your head. That's OK. You don't have to know a word to use it as the name of your company. Here we introduce you to several research tools to help you go beyond the words you know and generate lists of words that are novel, niche, or arcane. An odd word is OK. The purpose of a name isn't to create clarity; it is to create curiosity.

Step 5: Deciding on the Final Name

Here we take the work you did in Steps 2-4 and analyze it in terms of the rules you set out in Step 1. Remember, there is no gold standard for names. There is no governing body. There is only what you like, what will work for your business, and what will resonate with your customers.

You don't have to trust me that this is the best process. There is an often-cited 1995 study in the *Journal of Advertising Research* called "Creating Effective Brand Names: A Study of the Naming Process." The authors interviewed more than 100 brand managers responsible for product naming and developed the following five-step process[2]:

1. Establish objectives
2. Create a list of name candidates
3. Evaluate names
4. Choose final name

5. Submit name to PTO

This is pretty similar to the naming process in this book. However, it departs in two key ways. First, I have found that the second step is really hard. Most people can't just sit down and come up with a list of names. I broke that step out into three separate stages to help you develop the best name possible. The second change is that I combined the last three steps into one. In my experience, evaluating and choosing happen simultaneously. And the process of applying for patents and trademarks is complicated enough to deserve a side conversation. Some businesses won't need to be concerned with this at all. But for those that will, it is important enough to likely require legal expertise. (More about that later.)

At the risk of sounding overly philosophical, naming things is part of what it means to be human. We name children, pets, and plants. We name our cars. I even named a bicycle once. (OK, I've named several bicycles.) If we name things so prodigiously, why is naming a company so hard? For one, we don't do it very often. And we don't tend to develop processes for things we don't do often. This book gives you a process to get out of the rut George Vancouver found himself in.

Now it's time to get to work. This book is organized around a series of worksheets and brainstorming prompts and activities. I encourage you to use it as a workbook or journal as you move through the process. If you would rather do it on a spreadsheet or your own paper, that is fine. Everyone works differently. That said, it is important to go through the exercises in order. Each step builds on the one before it.

I would say "Good luck," but you don't need it. You are going to put in the work. It only looks like luck to others.

PREWRITING PRACTICE MAKES PERFECT

This book includes several exercises and brainstorms designed to help you find the best name for your business. That means I'm going to ask you to do a lot of writing. In my experience, it is hard for people to start writing about themselves. That's why I recommend that you do a bit of warmup by trying something a little easier—writing about other companies. Before you even begin moving through the steps of this book, it's important to get your brainstorming/writing brain in gear. Doing some prewriting like this will kick-start your critical thinking and get you used to writing on the page without constantly editing. It can be a little messy. After all, we haven't even dug into the actual steps yet. The pressure is off.

Writing like this may seem a little uncomfortable. That's because it's asking you to think critically about something you usually take for granted—company names. For this exercise, notice all the names around you. Start in the morning. You wake up. You might look at your phone. You go into the kitchen to grind coffee. You get your breakfast. You shower and brush your teeth. You put on your clothes. You gather your keys and briefcase and head to work.

You interacted with easily two dozen brand names in that brief process. The categories are pretty diverse:

+ Technology
+ Clothing
+ Food/beverage
+ Appliances
+ Soap/shampoo/toothpaste
+ Bike/car/transit

What is the history of the names in these categories that you see every day? What are they communicating to you? Levi's is named after its founder. Patagonia is named after an outdoor travel destination. Nike is the ancient Greek goddess of victory. What's the story behind Apple, Burt's Bees, and Starbucks? Who is the Tom from Tom's of Maine?

This exercise will help you think about how these words work as names. What do they mean? What do they sound like, look like, and feel like? Choose three companies. For each one, think of three possible meanings for the name. Then draw a conclusion about what those meanings might say about the business.

Here's an example:

Company Name: La Croix

Meaning: European sophistication

Meaning: French table water

Meaning: Some connection to cross?

Company names can have bizarre stories. I hear "La Croix," and because I know it translates to "the cross," I picture an order of French monks hand-bottling lightly flavored sparkling waters. In fact, it was started by a beer company in La Crosse, Wisconsin, in the early 1980s. Using the French translation of its town's name put it into the same league as rival water companies Perrier or San Pellegrino, though. And that's the point. Try the exercise for yourself.

Practice Round Exercise

Look around you and choose three brand names that you don't know much about. Write them down here. Next, speculate on what the names might mean. Write down your ideas. If you wish, spend some time looking into the history of each company. Their back story might inspire you.

Company Name _____

Meaning _____

Meaning _____

Company Name _____

Meaning _____

Meaning _____

Company Name _____

Meaning _____

Meaning _____

See? It's not so hard to write, right? Now that you're in the mode of brainstorming and writing; you're ready to move on to the first step of naming your company. Let's do this.

STEP 1

ESTABLISHING CRITERIA

Saying you want to name your business is like saying you want to go to Chicago. It's good you know where you want to go, but that isn't the only thing you need to know. To begin, you need to know how you are going to get there. Maybe you plan to drive. If so, you will need directions. If you just get in the car and start driving, you may end up in Sheboygan or Charlotte. You need to know when to get off the interstate and when to stay the course.

To continue this analogy, establishing criteria is like Google Maps. If you are very lucky or very good at navigating, you might get by without them. But most of us need that little voice saying, "In 1,000 feet, turn left."

Most of us aren't naturally great at naming. And we don't want to just trust in luck for something this important. This step is full of exercises that will help you decide on the criteria for your name and help focus your subsequent brainstorming efforts.

The most common mistake for people naming an organization is starting before they agree on criteria. If you don't have a shared set of standards by which you can judge whether a word will make a good name, all you have to fall back on is personal preference. And most people don't think about naming enough to rely on their preferences. You likely won't know why you like or dislike a certain word, and you definitely won't be able to leverage those feelings to create something new.

If you are working alone, setting criteria will save you from yourself. It will help you judge names more objectively and help you see your company from your customer's perspective. If you are working in a group, your criteria will help resolve arguments. They will enable you to make a solid group decision based on strategy, not arbitrary preferences.

As mentioned above, establishing criteria will also help focus your brainstorming efforts later. You will spend less time chasing down ideas that you know won't work. For example, if ease of pronunciation is one of your criteria, you will consider fewer words from other languages. If you want a name full of meaning, you won't waste time inventing words. So investing a little time now in establishing your criteria will save more time later and result in a better name.

In this step, you will learn how to establish your own naming criteria based on several factors. The first section discusses various hacks you can use to improve your name's memorability. We then look at tones, unwritten rules in your industry, meaning, unusualness, and spelling and pronunciation. By the end of this step, you will have a short list of criteria. That list will prove invaluable as you work your way toward finding a name. This step can sometimes feel like backtracking because you have been thinking about your business and its name for so long. Get your criteria out of your head and onto the paper (or screen). It is well worth the effort.

MEMORABILITY

A name has done its job if it causes a person to pause for a second. That said, the name is even more valuable if you can remember it long after that pause. Memorability matters. So how do you create a memorable name? In a 2003 article that appeared in the *Journal of Advertising*, "The Relation Between Brand-Name Linguistic Characteristics and Brand-Name Memory," the authors cited the following features as devices that enhance either the recall or recognition of brand names[1]:

+ Rhyme
+ Unusual spelling
+ Onomatopoeia
+ Initial hard consonant
+ Wordplay
+ Figurative language
+ Brand-name fit

These factors all enhance the memorability of a brand name, and they are most effective with new names. You won't want to use all of them. For some, the negatives (outlined later) will outweigh any potential benefit. The danger is that the names can feel contrived. Let's look at a few of them in greater detail, along with some other factors that influence memorability. You will want to keep these in mind as you develop your criteria.

Familiarity

This isn't in the above list, but it is worth acknowledging. The same *Journal of Advertising* article says that familiarity plays a larger role in brand-name memorability than the linguistic features of the name. Repetition is one of the most effective ways to make a name familiar. That is the idea behind advertising: repetition to create familiarity. So more familiar brand names are more memorable because we see them more often[2]. For example, AT&T is one of the largest spenders on advertising, year after year. In 2015 they spent nearly $3.9 billion on advertising in the U.S. I certainly remember the name, although it isn't inherently memorable. I would say it's even forgettable. But it is everywhere, from billboards to buses, on my telephone, and on TV. The brand achieves familiarity through ubiquity. So the more familiar a brand is, the less important linguistic devices are. The following are especially important considerations for new companies, which lack that familiarity. Though, as you will see, there are some pretty familiar companies that have used these devices, too.

Rhyme

Poets know this, and now you do, too: Rhyme aids in memory[3]. Think Coca-Cola. Or the infamous line, "If it doesn't fit, you must acquit." Nursery rhymes rhyme for a good reason—rhyming helps children (and adults) remember. For example, "Jack be nimble. Jack be quick. Jack jump over the candleholder" isn't as catchy as the line you might remember well, "Jack be nimble. Jack be quick. Jack jump over the candlestick."

While rhyme is common in many formats, it also works for brand names. This technique is especially common with consumer-facing brands. Here are a few examples:

+ Reese's Pieces
+ Lean Cuisine
+ Slim Jim

Many of the rhyming food names tend to be lower-cost, impulse items, often marketed to younger consumers. Slim Jim's most memorable campaign (which ran in the late 1990s) featured a professional wrestler, Macho Man Randy Savage. His line "Need a little excitement? Snap into a Slim Jim!" is still imprinted deeply into my brain. Lean Cuisine, however, shows that a company marketing to adults can still use this device without being cheeky.

Rhyming isn't restricted solely to food companies, either. Here is a range of companies using the device. They don't feel forced or gimmicky because the parts of the name are related to what they do. Consider these rhyming brands:

+ FireWire
+ StubHub
+ Crunch 'n Munch

Crunch 'n Munch gives you a hint at the texture and addictive nature of the treat. The rhyme of StubHub is almost a sentence. You get the idea that it is a place where you can buy tickets. And FireWire's rhyme is a metaphor: You get the sense that the wire transfers information fast. Rhyme can work for more grown-up businesses if the words give you valuable information about the business or product.

Unusual Spellings

Does *Kraft* stick with you more than the standard *Craft*? *Krispy Kreme* or *Crispy Cream*? Research says unusual spelling can make a name more memorable. Building on the previous point about rhyme, here are a couple of names that do both[4]:

+ Laffy Taffy
+ Mello Yello

The unusual spelling combined with the rhyme reinforces the youthful nature of the product and likely its memorability. Is Mello Yello more memorable than its competitor Mountain Dew? Likely.

There are unusual spellings everywhere you look. For example, Krispy Kreme feels like a nod back to a bygone era in product naming. So do Cheez Whiz and Chick-fil-A. That is because they were named in 1937, 1952, and 1967 respectively. This trend has recently become more common again, especially online. A scarcity of URLs spurred this trend among startups. Some examples include:

+ Digg
+ Flickr
+ Reddit

As more URLs became available, this trend has slowed. Is there space for you to use an unusual spelling purposefully? When Twitter launched, they were called "twttr" (without the vowels). Twitter.com was owned by someone else and they were part of a movement toward companies omitting vowels. That trend subsided, and they got large enough to buy the domain, so they changed their name to Twitter. There is a fine line between memorable and cute. And your brand may not want to be cute.

Onomatopoeia

This is a big word for a simple idea. Some words sound like what they represent: snap, crackle, pop, twitter. Picture the old *Batman* TV show. The word bubbles representing the various punches and kicks are onomatopoeia. Some brands use this tool, like the *zip* in Zipcar. Does that make it sound easier and quicker to use than its competitor, Car2go? What about Meow Mix? Would your cat like it better than Purina Cat Chow? It might be more memorable, especially with variations of the tag line: "Tastes so good, cats ask for it by name."[5]

Names that sound like what they represent tend to be more memorable. Ask yourself if this fits with what you are trying to create.

Initial Hard Consonant

According to research in reading studies, words starting with hard consonants (*t, k, p, d, g, v*) are more memorable than words starting with vowels or softer consonants[6]. They also are considered stronger.

In fact, recent studies indicate that the use of consonants and their placement can affect the perceived gender of a brand.

The sound of the consonant matters. Consider a spinoff company from Kraft Foods, Mondelez. Mondelez manages such brands as Cadbury, Chips Ahoy, Honey Maid, Toblerone, and Triscuit. According to their website, they "will lead the future of snacking around the world by offering the right snack, for the right moment, made the right way." The name Mondelez is a new word made from Latin parts like *mundus*, meaning world. It is intended to invoke the idea that there is a whole delicious world out there. However, compared to Kraft, "Mondelez" is decidedly forgettable. Of course, this is partly because it isn't as familiar, but research suggests it could be because of the weaker starting consonant, *m*. When I see the name, all I can think of is Mandalay Bay. I doubt they had Vegas in mind when deciding what to call the parent company of brands such as Oreo, Ritz, and Tang.

Wordplay (Puns)

A wordplay (or pun) is a type of joke that plays on the fact that some words sound similar but have very different meanings[7]. My 8-year-old sons have a joke book containing jokes all 8-year-olds should know. Other than bathroom jokes, the book is dominated by puns. And boy, do they remember them.

Some pun-inspired names are memorable for all the wrong reasons. In a quick search, I came across Bread Zeppelin, Wok This Way, and Nin Com Soup. I will never find out if they're real, because I would never go to these places. Tread carefully with puns unless you are going after the eight-year-old demographic.

Would you go to a bar called Tequila Mockingbird? Get your chair fixed at Wooden-It-Be-Nice? The names certainly catch your attention. They might even be memorable. But is that for the right reason? Does it illuminate the depth of their brand, or is it just a cheap gimmick? Maybe it's both.

Figurative Language

Figurative language is a way of saying something indirectly[8]. There are several types of figurative language, but we will focus here on metaphor and simile. Instead of saying that his eyes are blue, you can use a simile and say that his eyes are like the sea. Or, you can use a metaphor to describe her eyes as shining emeralds. The descriptions are similar, but by being indirect it is also much richer. Like rhyme, figurative language can make names more memorable. If your business is new, associating it with other meanings through the use of metaphor or simile can add richness and depth to a new name. This is important enough that this step includes a whole section on meaning. More on this later.

Brand Name Fit

Some names sound like they fit with the other names in an industry. These sorts of names tend to be more memorable. For example, in a 1998 *Journal of Marketing* article, "The Effects of Brand Name Suggestiveness on Advertising Recall," the authors claim the name "PicturePerfect Televisions" tests better for memorability than "Emporium Television." Why is that? PicturePerfect sounds more like the name of a TV brand than Emporium does. So meeting consumer expectations can be positive[9].

However, if you are thinking of using a name that defies expectations, this doesn't mean you shouldn't do it. You may have great reasons to break with tradition. But it is valuable to know that you will have to do something to combat the memorability problem. Maybe you could use the other memory devices discussed above. Maybe you will need to advertise more. Maybe you need great design, consumer reviews, or customer experience. There are many ways to compensate for a slight negative if you have a long-term positive in mind.

Memorability Exercise

When asked about naming his company Kodak, George Eastman said that the letter *k* "is a strong, incisive sort of letter." While he intuited this in the 1880s, you have the benefit of modern research to back up your decision. Intuition is important. If you like the name, other people might as well. But you don't have to rely on just your intuition. You can use rhyme, unusual spelling, onomatopoeia, initial hard consonants, wordplay, figurative language, and name brand fit to ensure your name is memorable.

You have seen several examples of companies that use these devices to make their names more memorable. They can give your name an advantage over your competition. Below, list three memorability enhancers you would consider using. Then brainstorm three additional company names that use each device.

Memorability Enhancer _____

Company _____

Company _____

Company _____

Memorability Enhancer _____

Company _____

Company _____

Company _____

Memorability Enhancer _____

Company _____

Company _____

Company _____

TONES

Your company has brand tones, even if you are just starting out. For example, if you are the company founder, your personality attributes might be the tones. They might describe you or early employees. They might describe your product or service. If you are an established business, the tones might represent your company's culture. If you haven't taken the time to think about your tones, do it now. Let's look at a few examples to clarify what we mean.

What might have been aspirational tones for us at Bullhorn when we started the company were "smart, irreverent, and hardworking." Because we didn't have a clearly defined product at the beginning, those tones were really describing me and my partner. In a sense, we *were* the product.

Those tones also apply to our name. The name doesn't have to explicitly state the tones; "Bullhorn" doesn't directly say "smart" or "irreverent." It's most important that the name doesn't conflict with your tones. "Bullhorn" isn't inconsistent with "hardworking." It might even imply it. It doesn't clash with "irreverent." It might bring to mind marching or labor organizing—that is certainly considered irreverent by the people in charge!

Here's another example. Say you are starting a new watch company, and your tones are "approachable" and "fun." "Montblanc" would be a bad choice for a name. It's exclusive and cold. It is literally a snow-covered mountain climbable by only a few. You could rule out that name because it directly contradicts your tones. However, if it's fun you're going for, something like "Shinola" might be a great choice.

Tones can be found everywhere in your business. Ask yourself questions about your company, like:

+ How do you talk about yourselves?
+ How do you paint the walls?
+ How would you describe the office décor?
+ What does your product feel like?

The words you use to answer questions like these can help you identify words that describe you. Here are a few possibilities, but please don't limit yourself to these:

+ Sleek
+ Chic
+ Modern
+ Traditional
+ Artisanal
+ Approachable
+ Exclusive
+ High-end
+ Democratic
+ Timeless
+ Current

You can see that some of these tones fit together well, while others are at odds. For example, it is hard to imagine a business that is both approachable and exclusive. If the name is approachable, it is likely to be more colloquial or comfortable. It is friendly. Think about a name like Home Depot. It is familiar. It sounds like a place you could visit in whatever you happen to be wearing. No need to dress up.

That's not the case if the tone is exclusive, however. The name might be colder or foreign-sounding because exclusivity is based on the idea of distance. It is something you aspire to but might not quite achieve. With an exclusive tone, the name should remain just out of reach for the average consumer. The most obvious examples come from fashion: Louis Vuitton, Versace, Dior. These names, for English speakers, maintain distance due to pronunciation barriers and historical associations with the upper classes.

Tones Exercise

Now that you see the importance of tones, make a list of ten or more potential tones that describe your company. Try to make each one as different as possible. It might help to imagine how someone might characterize you or the co-worker everyone loves, or how a customer might describe your business. Combine similar concepts or eliminate anything that doesn't work. You want to end up with a final list of five tones.

Tone _____

Tone _____

Tone _____

Tone _____

Tone _____

Tone _____

Tone _____

Tone _____

Tone _____

Tone _____

Tone _____

Tone _____

Tone _____

Tone _____

Tone _____

UNWRITTEN RULES

Every industry has a set of unwritten branding rules, or tendencies that become codified over time. Sometimes they can become clichés. Most industries will have only a couple of types of names. This happens naturally. One company finds success, and the next company mimics them because it worked for the first. The next thing you know, it is a rule, and no one remembers why it started. This applies to everything from how businesses are run to color choice and typography to their names. But let's look at naming for now.

Bullhorn is a good example. There are general naming trends in the branding agency world that have become unwritten rules. The first is to use a modifier with the word "brand," like this:

+ Moving Brands
+ Interbrand
+ FutureBrand

I chose these companies because they are all large, successful agencies that do great work. In many ways, they are the agencies Bullhorn aspires to be. But their names are forgettable. More than that, they are undifferentiated. How could you remember if you liked the work from Moving, Inter, or Future? The names are too similar.

The second general trend is the law firm model, in which you name the agency after the founder(s), like this:

+ Landor
+ Lippincott
+ Wolff Olins

While these names are unique, they don't tell you much about the company. What they *do* is give historical weight. They sound established. They sound old. Choosing this sort of name puts you in the same tier as other professional service providers—hence the "law firm model" description. What these names tell consumers is that the providers will tend to be safe, traditional, and fairly expensive choices.

We also looked at advertising agencies because they often have branding capabilities. Many ad agencies start with the law firm model until the name gets too long and unwieldy. At that point they make it an initialism, like this:

+ WPP
+ BBDO
+ DDB

Again, I am picking on these three because they are massive, global companies that do the most recognizable work in their industry. They can take it. These names are undeniably easier to handle, but they're interchangeable.

So we have identified three general naming trends among our competitors: modifier with "brand," law firm model, and initialism. The important thing is what to do with this information. I'm assuming that if you want a name like everyone else in your industry, you wouldn't be reading this book.

For Bullhorn, we didn't want the name to have the word "brand" in it. We also didn't want to name it after the founders. This is partly because when you google my last name you get a bunch of flower shops, but that is beside the point. And finally, we didn't want a name that would eventually become an initialism. Those tend to be forgettable, especially for a new company that doesn't have the benefit of familiarity.

As we discussed in the section on memorability above, there is a limit to how far outside the unwritten rules you can go. People tend to prefer names that sound like they fit in their category[10]. But if the name is too similar to all the other companies, it will blend in with the noise. And if you go too far in the other direction, it won't be recognized as something that fits.

Fortunately, "Bullhorn" still makes sense here. While in the minority, metaphorical names are still used in the branding space, and often to great effect. Consider these examples, all branding agencies like Bullhorn:

+ Matchstic
+ Salt
+ Murmur

These companies are using metaphors in a way that is similar to our logic. Maybe Matchstic creates the spark that starts the fire. Salt provides the seasoning that makes your brand delicious. Murmur is using a similar metaphor from an opposite perspective. It is also about communication, but they aren't yelling it in your face. They are creating the word-of-mouth that travels from person to person. Thus, Murmur.

So it is important to think about your industry. Like ours, yours will likely have a few unwritten rules. What are they, and why do they exist? Can you break some of them and stand out from the crowd, or is there a good reason to follow them? Do you want to be perceived as established or as an upstart? That perception is greatly influenced by how you choose to position yourself in relation to your industry's unwritten rules.

Unwritten Rules Exercise

Make a list of 30 or so of your competitors. It might help to divide them into groups. What are the most established companies in your industry? Which companies are disrupting tradition? Are there outliers that are just strange? Once you've identified your groups, you can pick out three naming trends. Circle the trends you are interested in pursuing, and cross out the ones you want to avoid.

Trend 1 _____

Trend 2 _____

Trend 3 _____

MEANING

When thinking about the meaning of your name, there are two clear paths. You can choose a real word or phrase, and your name will have its meaning built in. A real word like "apple" is like a packed suitcase. It comes with stuff. You may like some of it; there are other parts you may not appreciate. There are many reasons to choose a real word. It is more recognizable. It sets a firmer foundation for the rest of the brand language, such as the tag line and headlines, because you are working with the familiar images and references the word brings to the table.

The other path is to choose a made-up word. Names like Twilio, Zillow, and Skype don't really mean anything. They are more like an empty bucket. You get to fill it with what you want. But that can take more time and effort. You might choose a name like this if you were in a highly competitive industry and needed a trademark. You might also invent a name if you needed to stand out. The lack of familiarity with the word causes the consumer to pause. In that pause, you have a chance to tell your own story.

Meaning in naming is complicated. To understand its subtleties, let's explore the three main types of meaning: literal, metaphorical, and associative. We'll continue using Apple as the example so you can see how the three types differ.

Literal Meaning

Imagine what that hypothetical first day in the life of Apple might have been like. The paperwork is filed with the secretary of state. The company is official. Steve Jobs goes out to get a drink to celebrate, and the person at the bar next to him asks why he is so happy.

Steve: *I just started a company.*

Stranger: *Cool. What are you going to do?*

Steve: *Make computers you will actually want to use.*

Stranger: *Nice! What's it called?*

Steve: *Apple Computer.*

Stranger: *Apple? Like, the fruit?*

Steve: *Yeah. You know, it's a metaphor.*

Stranger: *A metaphor? Do y'all work for an orchard or something?*

Steve: *No, we are going to change the world.*

Stranger: *With fruit?*

You get the idea. When a company doesn't have much history, the consumer's first instinct is to think literally. This is because many business names are descriptive. Bob owns a car wash, so of course, it is called Bob's Car Wash. A day care is located in Chevy Chase, Maryland—and yes, its name is Chevy Chase Day Care. These names are so common we hardly notice them—especially for local businesses. The literal definition of a word is likely the first thing you will think of. Clearly it is important. But you can also use the literal meaning of a word to make a name interesting.

Elon Musk's The Boring Company does this. It is literally boring holes in the earth. Once you know what they do, the double entendre gives the name enough edge to be engaging. The holes—tunnels— are used to transport you and your vehicle across town. The name is certainly not boring in the common sense: uninteresting, tedious.

Literal names can work, but be careful. They can also be a little obvious, and therefore forgettable. Even if the customer does remember your name, a generic name can be difficult to find afterward.

If you go down this road, think about how to create your own twist on the name to stand out.

Metaphorical Meaning

After the first encounter with a name, take time to reflect and consider why it was chosen. In the case of Apple, the company isn't being literal; they are using a metaphor—a word that stands for something other than the surface meaning. Metaphor adds richness. This can work really well for young businesses. A metaphor can add shades of meaning to a company that is starting with nothing. It can be a suitcase full of useful stuff. If you are renaming an existing organization, a metaphor can also help indicate a change of intent.

For example, we have a client called Broomwagon, a startup bike shop/coffee shop. It could have been given a literal name like Tiff's Bikes, but that doesn't really tell you much. Their customers are bike insiders, who know that the broom wagon is a vehicle that follows behind a bike race. Its job is to pick up the riders who have fallen off the pace. So the shop is aimed at bike insiders, but not the hardcore ones who imagine themselves at the front of the race.

The name Broomwagon conveys quite a bit before their doors even open. It tells you the owners think about things differently from a traditional bike shop. It hints that they might be more laid-back. It is a place where you can get coffee and a pastry in the morning and then stick around and drink a beer with your lunch. You can assume their bike and parts selection is geared to a less hardcore segment of the cycling crowd—more commuters than racers. They carry more hooded sweatshirts than spandex jerseys. The helmets aren't aerodynamic, but they have a place to attach a flashing light for safety on the roads. You can even buy a mallet for an emerging sport called bike polo. All these decisions point back to a name that says, "We aren't at the front of the race, but we still enjoy riding our bicycle, and we will support you so that you can, too."

Now back to Apple. What metaphors come to mind? Do you think of Sir Isaac Newton and the apple that allegedly inspired his revelation? Do you think of Eve eating from the tree of knowledge? Look at the logo: an apple with a bite out of it. (Or look at the original Apple logo, used for only a year in 1976: an old-fashioned drawing of Newton reading under a tree.) Either metaphor speaks to the culture of the company:

+ Empowering individuals
+ Powering breakthroughs
+ Curiosity
+ Fresh ideas
+ Inspiration

Metaphorical meaning is an important consideration. As you prepare for the following exercise, think about the list above. In the same way that Apple speaks to curiosity, what elements of your company culture can be conveyed metaphorically? What secondary meanings might a name or phrase have for your customers?

Metaphorical Meaning Exercise

How are other companies using metaphors successfully? List ten companies using metaphors in their names. With each name, draw some conclusions about what they are trying to convey. In the Apple example, the company hasn't directly stated those meanings. They have been written and speculated about widely.

Metaphor name _____

Meaning _____

Meaning _____

Meaning _____

Metaphor name _____

Meaning _____

Meaning _____

Meaning _____

Metaphor name _____

Meaning _____

Meaning _____

Meaning _____

ASSOCIATIVE MEANING

Apple and its logo are ubiquitous. In a sense, they are post-name. In other words, the apple symbol is so prominent that they rarely use the name. In fact, the company name isn't even on the homepage of their website. Just the icon. If you go to one of their product pages, you won't see the name on the main page header, just the icon. You might even call it the *Mac* store, a reference to a product, rather than the company itself.

Today, the name "Apple" has *associative* meaning, or the connection of nonlinear ideas. You wouldn't normally associate an apple with a phone. But now the name has wide association beyond its literal or metaphorical meaning. It is the phone in your pocket, your library of music, and your computer. It is a certain type of person in a coffee shop. It even stands for the creative office cliché: a long row of matte-silver monitors.

Associative meaning happens naturally to companies over time. A company name starts out as literal or figurative. As the company becomes more established, the name's meaning becomes conflated with the services it provides or the products it sells. The name can become associated with the people who work there or the places where they work. In other words, a name's ability to develop associative meaning is organic.

You don't have to wait for this to happen naturally over time. You can play on associative meaning as a startup. Here's an example. 37 Signals is the original name of a web development company that created Basecamp, a project management and team communication software platform. According to their origin story, there have been 37 instances of soundwaves from outer space that haven't been identified. 37 Signals makes sense literally, though it might be a little confusing to the outsider. It also might be a metaphor if you are thinking of signal vs. noise and creating meaning. It also might be associative. The name associates the company with the search for communication with the unknown.

What associative meaning do you want your company's name to have? Here are just a few possibilities:

+ Transportation
+ Exploration
+ Knowledge
+ Famous educators
+ Famous healers
+ Warriors
+ Musicians
+ Athletes
+ Vacation destinations
+ Hard work
+ Relaxation

Choose wisely. Your name—and the meaning associated with it—will be with you for a while.

Associative Meaning Exercise

Think a little about the brand names around you. What do the names mean, and how is that different from the things you associate with

CASE STUDY
Coca-Cola

As you can see, a name's meaning is an important, multilayered consideration that can change over time. It is rooted in the history of the company. How does this work in real life? Let's consider an example, and as you read, imagine this is your brand's origin story.

It is the summer of 1865, and it is oppressively hot. A Confederate officer has just participated in one of the most gruesome events in American history. He is tired, discouraged, and generally depressed as he rides slumped on his horse home to Georgia after the war. He sustained a saber wound in battle and was given morphine to manage the pain.

But the morphine habit proves difficult to shake. He finally pulls himself out of bed to visit the druggist, determined to ditch the opiate. Together, they come up with an elixir that is a combination of alcohol and stimulants. It tastes pretty good and makes him feel great. Maybe other people would be interested in it, too.

Unfortunately, the temperance movement is gaining momentum in the South, so he goes back to the druggist to come up with a nonalcoholic version. The final product is a combination of carbonated water, sugar, spices, caffeine, and (a special guest) cocaine. It doesn't take the edge off the pain quite as well, but it still gets you out of bed in the morning.

He decides to name it Coca-Cola. Coca from the coca leaves that provide the cocaine, and Cola from the kola nut that supplies the caffeine. It's touted as a "brain tonic" that is "exhilarating and invigorating."

Unfortunately, as the product goes to market, the inventor retreats to his sick bed. He sells off the remainder of his stock to sustain his stubborn morphine addiction and dies shortly thereafter. It's not the kind of inspirational story you'd want to use as the anchor for a growing company.

CASE STUDY, CONT.

So the company's success can't rest on its origin story or on the literal meaning of its name, which is mostly negative.

The name took on an additional negative connotation about 100 years later. I grew up in the 1980s. One of the prominent TV commercials was by the Partnership for a Drug-Free America. The ad showed a person holding an egg and saying, "This is your brain." They crack the egg in a hot pan and say, "This is your brain on drugs."

It was clear and to the point. At the time, a primary social concern was the dramatic increase in cocaine use. Powdered cocaine was used by rich people, and poorer people used the rock form called crack. When the egg was cracked on the television it was hard not to think of coke, a shorthand for cocaine. Unfortunately, Coca-Cola had also been shortened to Coke by this time.

But the company was going gangbusters by that point. You would think the total baggage of the name would be impossible to overcome, but we didn't blink. When asked what we want to drink, we often mechanically say, "I'll have a Coke." In some parts of the United States, "Coke" (not soda or pop or soda pop) is shorthand for any carbonated soft drink.

But why? There are several answers to that question. One is that "Coca-Cola" sounds great. It has a poetic cadence. The repetition of the long o sounds gives the name a buoyancy that mimics the carbonation of the drink. The hard k sounds balance that buoyancy with confidence. The rhyme of the words makes the name more memorable. It sounds refreshing. Even when shortened to Coke, it is good. It has brevity and acceleration. It ends with a hard stop. It is self-contained and solid, where the effervescent "Pepsi" floats away.

Negative literal meaning. A strange history. Negative cultural connotations. An origin related to poor health outcomes. And still it is one of the most valuable brands in the world.

CASE STUDY, CONT.

My point is that meaning matters when naming your company, but it isn't everything. There are multiple factors to take into consideration. Is the name memorable? Does it sound nice? Is it unusual?

them? For example, Dyson vacuum cleaners are named after the company's founder, James Dyson. I don't at all associate the name with him, though. I associate it with the strange, inventive vacuums that broke with traditional designs. List three companies you encounter in your daily life. What do you associate them with? Was the name designed that way, or was it something that happened organically over time? List each one here, along with the meanings you think of when you hear or see the brand name.

Brand name _____

Meaning _____

Meaning _____

Meaning _____

Brand name _____

Meaning _____

Meaning _____

Meaning _____

Brand name _____

Meaning _____

Meaning _____

Meaning _____

UNUSUALNESS

Most people assume they want an unusual brand or company name. You can achieve that in different ways: by using foreign or misspelled words, for example, or by combining uncommon words, as in the case of Coca-Cola (see sidebar, above).

Deciding how unusual a name you need is the first criterion. That is because unusualness is faceted. The last section described meaning as a spectrum, from literal to figurative. Unusualness can also be thought of as a spectrum. On one end is a novel word (Hulu); on the other is a common word (Mama). Either pole can work, but the best choice for you might land somewhere in the middle.

To make it even more complicated, there is competition to use individual words as names. Regardless of how common or uncommon they are, some companies have the same or similar names. But is this a problem?

For example, Delta Air Lines and Delta Faucet Co. are both leaders in their industries. The word "delta" is recognizable but isn't commonly used in everyday speech. Some people might identify it as a Greek letter, while others may understand its mathematical meaning. But it is still fairly obscure.

So the two Deltas have identical names. Is that a problem? Probably not, because you wouldn't confuse the airline with the faucet manufacturer. The identical names still provide a unique identity for both of them because they do not cause confusion in the marketplace.

Delta Air Lines stands out among its peers: American, United, KLM, Southwest. Similarly, Delta stands out among other faucet manufacturers: Kohler, American Standard, Moen. And I didn't even address Delta Dental, the insurance company.

Breyer's and Dreyer's is another example. Clearly, the names are similar. They are in the same industry; they both make ice cream. And their industry is hyper-competitive. Is there the potential for confusion? Imagine taking a grocery order over the phone. Are you certain the customer asked for Breyer's? In this case, both companies would benefit from more distinctive names.

So how do you determine how unusual your name should be?

Advertising

The first way to gauge how unusual your name needs to be is to assess how much advertising your competition does. Generally, whatever is advertised—company or product—has higher name competitiveness. It isn't as important for Procter & Gamble to have an uncommon name as it is for Crest toothpaste. It doesn't matter if the publisher of this book has a name that stands out, as long as the book's title does.

Think about your industry. Are you a local wealth manager? While that business is competitive, there isn't as much name competition as in other industries. Your competition likely advertises less than, say, someone selling supplements online.

Geography and Competition

The second consideration is geography. What is your geographic footprint? Does your organization plan to serve a neighborhood, a town, or an urban metro area? Are you serving a statewide audience, or is your reach national or even international? Are you starting a massage therapy business or a restaurant chain? Where you operate matters. The smaller your geographic footprint, the less competition you will have, and the less emphasis you will need to place on an unusual name.

For example, say you're starting a company that manufactures and sells a supplement. This particular supplement takes fat cells and reallocates them into your wrinkles, so you get skinnier and your skin looks younger. You notice that online, print, and television advertising are saturated with health and wellness products. So you can assume there will be significant competition. You decide to sell your product through your website and in specialty retailers, so your geographic footprint is potentially international. With heavy advertising and a broad geographic footprint, your product's name will need to be quite unusual, for two reasons. One, you don't want to get sued for infringing on another company's trademark. And two, you want your fantastic youthening supplement to stand out among all the clutter.

Or consider a counterexample. You decide to start a nonprofit to help underprivileged children in your neighborhood prepare for college. These kids are all first-generation college students. They may not have successful study behavior patterns modeled for them, since they are the first in their families to go to college. Your organization is there to help them navigate life, give them a road map, and provide orientation before they go off to college. You will not have much competition. Small nonprofits like this may not advertise in the traditional sense. And your geographic footprint is constrained to your immediate neighborhood. This organization doesn't need an unusual name. You could look at common nouns—maybe something like Compass. It would likely need a modifier: perhaps Compass College Prep. There are certainly many businesses with the word *compass* in their names. But in this case, would it matter?

As you work through your criteria, unusualness is an important consideration. It determines how deep you will need to go later and what sorts of names you need to focus on. If you need your name to be extremely uncommon, you will spend more time working on made-up words, like Hulu, or digging into obscure words. The following exercise will help you determine where you fall on the unusualness spectrum.

Unusualness Exercise

Consider your company's requirements by reviewing the following criteria. Circle a number between 1–5 for each question.

1. How much competition will your business have?
   (1: I won't have any – 5: Super-competitive)

1 2 3 4 5

2. How much does your competition spend on advertising?
   (1: $ – 5: $$$$$)

1 2 3 4 5

3. What is your likely geographic footprint?
   (1: Local – 5: International)

1 2 3 4 5

Add up your total number of points for all three questions. If you have more than ten points in total, you should consider adding unusualness to your list of criteria at the end of this step. If not, don't worry too much about finding an uncommon name. You are lucky enough to work in a less-competitive industry.

SPELLING AND PRONUNCIATION

Spelling and pronunciation are important factors for any good name. If you are saying your name all day on the phone, pronunciation becomes pretty important. If your customers need to write or type your name frequently, spelling might matter more. You will get very tired of spelling your name every time you tell someone your email or snail-mail address if it is difficult or has a nonstandard spelling. But that is really only an issue over the phone.

We have a client in third-party logistics called Longship. If you are a company in Florida with a truckload of bananas, you would call Longship to get them to the distributor in Minnesota. They are on the phone constantly. Within the first minute in their office, you will hear someone say "This is Longship," 20 times. So ease of pronunciation was vital when they chose their company name. They must also call each truck driver to coordinate pickup and delivery. The driver has to fill out paperwork each time for both parties to get paid, so it was also important that the name be easy to spell.

That isn't always the case. There are times when misspellings work, and are even favorable. When URLs were scarce, for example, companies named themselves Flickr, Digg, or Dribbble. In my opinion, those are some of the best misspelled-on-purpose names. As more URLs become available, this is less of a concern. Names among startups (while still often bizarre) are now less likely to use intentional misspellings.

There might also be times when you *want* a name to be difficult to pronounce. Perhaps you can confidently pronounce Yves Saint Laurent (YSL). I cannot. But that's OK. Maybe it's strategic. Does the French name make it sound fashionable? Expensive? It does to me. The name works because it is aspirational. YSL currently sells a $12,500 sequined, double-breasted blazer. I am not the sort of guy who could buy that jacket, so it's a little beside the point to speculate on whether or not I would. But a name like Saint Laurent makes me want to, even if I am a little embarrassed to admit it.

Lululemon also uses difficult pronunciation to its advantage. It has been reported that Lululemon's founder engineered his athletic clothing line to be popular in Japan. A big part of that plan was to make the name sound more American. Since *l* isn't a sound native to Japanese speakers, it's difficult for them to pronounce. Hence, it sounds more American and more appealing. That might not make you like the company more, but it is an interesting naming strategy.

There are other ways to use difficult pronunciation. You may want your name to stand out. For example, there is no clear way to pronounce the name *Uniqlo*. Is it *you-nee-klo* or the softer-sounding *you-nih-klo*? The name is a new word derived from the phrase "Unique Clothing." Though you would never know that in context. In a mall or on a crowded street with dozens of other signs, maybe the nonstandard spelling is a plus. You have to stop for a second to think about it, and that is long enough to notice the clothing.

So think about the future. Is it more important for your company to have a name that is easy to spell and say, or is there a strategic reason you might want it to be more difficult?

Spelling and Pronunciation Exercise

Make a list of eight company names that are either misspelled or difficult to spell. Why do you think they made this choice? Is it beneficial or detrimental to the company?

Company _____

   – Why did they choose this spelling? _____

   – Does it help or hurt? _____

Company _____

   – Why did they choose this spelling? _____

   – Does it help or hurt? _____

Company _____

   – Why did they choose this spelling? _____

   – Does it help or hurt? _____

Company _____

  – Why did they choose this spelling? _____

  – Does it help or hurt? _____

Company _____

  – Why did they choose this spelling? _____

  – Does it help or hurt? _____

Company _____

  – Why did they choose this spelling? _____

  – Does it help or hurt? _____

Company _____

  – Why did they choose this spelling? _____

  – Does it help or hurt? _____

Company _____

  – Why did they choose this spelling? _____

  – Does it help or hurt? _____

SOUND

I had a creative writing professor in college who taught poetry. He talked about word choice and the importance of being concise and precise. He talked about discipline. It could just as easily have been a marketing course about messaging or a course about naming. The principles of clear, aesthetically pleasing communication apply across disciplines. That includes how we feel about sound.

As we discussed earlier, sound improves memorability through the use of devices like onomatopoeia, rhyme, and consonant use. But there is an additional aesthetic consideration when we talk about sound.

Often synonyms shouldn't be used interchangeably. My professor's example was the word "stone." In a thesaurus, "stone" and "rock" are synonymous. But they aren't, really. How a word sounds matters. Sound changes meaning. "Stone" starts soft with the *s* and finishes soft with the *n*, which lingers. It is smooth and liquid. In contrast, rock starts rougher. The *r* sound comes from the back of the throat in a near growl. The word ends with the abrupt *ck*. It is jagged.

In the song "Temporary Like Achilles," the songwriter Bob Dylan suggests the difference, talking about his advances on a woman and her dismissive attitude toward him. When describing her, he uses the words "stone" and "rock" in contrast. Her heart might be stone or rock, but not both.

It is important to note that one isn't better than the other; rock isn't necessarily better than stone, nor is a stone better than a rock. It is the difference that you want to acknowledge. The difference is connotation.

Sound matters in made-up words, too. For example, Esso spent millions of dollars to become Exxon. Due to a complex legal situation, the company was able to use Esso in some markets, Enco in others, and Humble in others. This caused practical business problems and general brand confusion. Esso changed the name because it was a business necessity. But they changed it to Exxon because it sounds stronger and more authoritative. In essence, they changed from *stone* to *rock*.

MODIFIERS VS. TAG LINES

Modifiers and tag lines are both mechanisms that add clarity to your company's name in the transitional period after you introduce the name but before it is established through repetition.

A *modifier* is a word or phrase that adds clarity to a word that might otherwise have been too general or misunderstood. The name "Central Bank" needs the modifier "bank" because "central" is so generic it could apply to just about any business. Wells Fargo is in the same industry, but their name is distinctive enough to stand on its own, without any modifiers. Over time, through repetition, familiarity wins out and modifiers are often dropped: Time Warner Cable became Time Warner, colloqially. Apple Computer became Apple.

A *tag line* is not actually part of the name: It is a longer phrase that clarifies the function of the business, and is more easily and commonly changed as the business's offerings change. If this seems confusing, that's because it is. There is no clear delineation between tag lines, slogans, mantras, or any of the other business buzzwords currently in vogue. I am not talking here about Apple's "Think Different" or Nike's "Just Do It." Those speak more to the company's culture than its purpose. When you have a new name, culture isn't generally your main concern. You are worried that no one will know what you do. If you decide on the bold name "Achilles" for your new business, it is comforting to know that you can add a tag line reading "The Strongest Name in Home Security." That clarifies what your company does and allows you to make a more daring name choice, knowing you will have an opportunity to explain it. The chief benefit of using a tag line is that it makes your core name simpler. But it is also much easier to change. All you have to do to change a tag line is reprint your business cards and edit your website. Changing your name, however, is a little more complex.

PERSONAL PREFERENCES

Inevitably, you will prefer certain types of names to others. And your preferences will be different from mine. You have thought of your company or product as a real thing for a while now and have probably pictured your business in a certain way. Ask yourself:

+ Do you want a name that means something or nothing?
+ Do you want it to be short?
+ Do you want it to start with a certain letter?
+ Do you want it to be a real word or made up?
+ Do you want the URL to be the same as the name?

Your preferences might be irrational or arbitrary, but that is OK. Humans are often irrational. What is most important to you in a name?

In order to generate the best name possible, it's important that you add any preference you have to your criteria. Once you look at it written down on paper, you may realize it is irrational and dismiss it. Or you may acknowledge it is a legitimate concern and add it to the tool that will help you pick your name.

The criterion may be something we have already discussed. Or it might be a preference for a particular type of name. We will work on name types in Step 3. As you go through the name-generating process in that step, you can always come back to this stage and add criteria.

So far, we have talked about what you like. There are also probably names you hate. There might even be whole categories of names you dislike. I certainly have mine. Generally, I want you to keep an open mind and see what you come up with. But if there are types of names you would never consider, write them down. This exercise is designed to help you articulate these preferences. What names do you love? What do you hate?

Personal Preferences Exercise

To determine your preferences, you will need to ask yourself some pointed questions. You may have never considered these issues before.

Think about some names that you hate. What do these names have in common? There may be a trend. Now do the same with some names you love. What do those names have in common? At the end of Step 1, we will add these results to your criteria list.

What are five business names that you hate?

Business: _____

Business: _____

Business: _____

Business: _____

Business: _____

What do those names have in common?

_____

_____

_____

_____

_____

What are five business names that you love?

Business: _____

Business: _____

Business: _____

Business: _____

Business: _____

What do those names have in common?

_____

_____

_____

_____

_____

CASE STUDY
Evol Foods

There are few places that compete for your attention like the grocery store. In my local store, there are 25 freezers just for ice cream and other frozen desserts—more than a thousand options. It's a similar story with toothpaste. It's even hard to choose toilet paper: single roll, double roll, mega roll, two-ply, quilted, ultra-strong, and so on.

One day I was at the store looking for a reasonable lunch option for my kids. Staring into one of the freezers next to all the ice cream, I came across a company called Evol that claimed to sell healthy frozen food. The name caught my attention, the tag line appealed to my sensibilities, and I suspected my kids would eat the burritos. So I bought some.

"Evol" is a strange name, but let's take a look at how they designed the logo. The e is backwards, while the other letters are symmetrical, so your brain automatically flips it around to read "love," a word I am sure the company could not trademark.

CASE STUDY, CONT.

Still, it's definitely odd—but that's why it works. Let's examine it in terms of the criteria you read about in this chapter.

Meaning. It is clear that they want you to see "love." But their tag line (which you can see on their website at https://www.evolfoods.com/), "Good is Evol," makes it obvious that it also sounds like "evil." So which is it? Maybe they're simply trying to point out that frozen foods are usually junk and theirs is wholesome. But that's a bit of a stretch. So the meaning is ultimately ambiguous and confusing.

Unusualness. I would guess this was top priority. They needed something that stood out. They also likely needed a URL that was short and available. Their market is saturated with advertising; they sell across the United States and potentially beyond. So an uncommon name is a key element to Evol's success.

Spelling and pronunciation. Difficult spelling is the tradeoff for the unique URL, but this can be irritating in practice. For example, every time employees mention the company email address, they probably have to spell it: "My address is brad@evol.com. No, evol with an o. E-V-O-L." That must get pretty tedious. There's also a pronunciation issue. Do you say it like the first part of "evolve" or does it sound like "evil"? Ambiguous pronunciation is a barrier. If you are too self-conscious to say a product's name, you are less likely to ask for it. However, here, you take the product off the shelf yourself. So maybe it works. But would you tell a friend about it?

Tones. Evol doesn't publish brand guidelines, but I would imagine its tones are something like vibrant, wholesome, and smart. That comes through in its name and branding.

CASE STUDY, CONT.

Bottom line. I wouldn't have named the company Evol. I find it gimmicky and self-conscious. I also think the pronunciation mix-up with evil outweighs the other interesting things the name does. But the name is still the main reason I bought the burritos. I paused for a second in front of the freezer doors, skimming past hundreds of available products, and looked at that particular product again. That is a home run. How many times have you bought a product because of the name? Probably not many. So the question is, does it matter that I don't like the name if it works? Probably not. Kudos to them for a bold choice.

What do you think?

CRITERIA LIST BRAINSTORM

Review the exercises in Step 1. Make a list of 5-10 criteria. Write a short description of each criterion to make it easier to remember when you use this list in the final step to decide on your name.

Criteria 1 _____

_____

Criteria 2 _____

_____

Criteria 3 _____

_____

CRITERIA LIST BRAINSTORM

Criteria 4 _____

_____

Criteria 5 _____

_____

Criteria 6 _____

_____

Criteria 7 _____

_____

Criteria 8 _____

_____

Criteria 9 _____

_____

Criteria 10 _____

_____

STEP 1 TAKEAWAYS ⟶

If you just skimmed Step 1 shaking your head, I get it. You are busy. There are a million things you have to do, and the last thing you need is an exercise about associative meaning, whatever that is. Here are the five main things you really need to know before you continue on:

1. If you don't take the time to set your criteria, you will have no way to create potential names, and if you do come up with some words, you will have no way to decide between them. Setting criteria is absolutely essential.

2. There are seven devices for enhancing memorability: rhyme, unusual spelling, onomatopoeia, initial hard consonant, word-play, figurative language, and brand-name fit. But remember, they are like salt. Too much and the dish is ruined. So choose your devices wisely.

3. Decide what tones represent your brand and what unwritten rules guide your industry. One will help with your name internally; the other will make sure you are repeating well-worn ideas.

4. Meaning is on a spectrum from a literal meaning to an associative meaning. Unusualness can range from a new word to a common one. Spelling and pronunciation can range from familiar to foreign. There are legitimate reasons to be placed anywhere along those axes. But you should choose your location purposefully.

5. Lastly, a tag line or modifier can leave you free to pick a bold name because you will be able to include explanatory notes while people get used to it.

STEP 2

BRAINSTORMING

There is a book called *Creative Confidence: Unleashing the Creative Potential Within Us All* by Tom and David Kelley[1]. The authors are brothers, business partners, and experts in creativity. David founded the design firm Ideo. He also went on to found the design institute at Stanford University, colloquially called the d.school. In the book, they use a pottery class to highlight how the creative process works. A pottery teacher wanted to figure out how good work was done, so he split the class in half. The first half would be graded on the quality of just one piece. The second half would be graded on quantity. How many pieces could they make during the course of the class? Fifty pounds of work was an A, 40 pounds was a B, and so on. Despite the fact that the first group of students had all semester to master one piece, the second group of students made not only the most work, but also the best work.

It's the same with names. People who spend all their time looking for just the right name will likely end up with very few options, and they won't be great. The people who spend their time generating lots of ideas will come up with the most interesting range of names and the best final choice. It's like a gold miner. The person who finds gold is the one down in the stream sifting through all the dirt and rock, not the one on the edge waiting to spot that gleam of gold in the water. In other words, focus less on perfection and more on production.

Most things we do revolve around getting the right answer. This is called *convergent thinking*. It is the type of thinking you learn in school when you are given a test, or at work when you are asked for a recommendation. In this type of thinking, you focus on conducting analysis to reach the "correct" answer. What you will practice here, though, is called *divergent thinking*. You are looking for lots of possible answers, not the one correct answer. Divergent thinking is about generating ideas.

This step is all about brainstorming, so it should come as no surprise that you will finish with several lists of words. These lists are the raw materials from which you will create your name. Remember: You are not looking for the right answer here. You are looking for lots of ideas. This step focuses on getting the ideas out of your head and onto paper, where you can work with them. It is meant to be a survey course in how to brainstorm and will help you get going on generating ideas. So you'll see that the following sections are focused on action and include several different ways to get your ideas down on paper.

It isn't immediately obvious how to start brainstorming. You start this step by getting really concrete. First, write five factual sentences about your business. Using those sentences, explore a few exercises. The first exercise is based around the verbs in the sentences. You then use those verbs as the starting point for brainstorms. The second exercise is centered on the objects in the sentences. And, yes, don't worry—there will be a brief grammar review. (I had to look up "object," too.) The object brainstorm starts off with nouns and tends to generate the most concrete words.

The second half of Step 2 gets a bit more abstract. Write five more sentences, this time using more figurative language. After reviewing the difference between metaphors and similes, you will use those pieces of less literal language to generate different sorts of words.

A note to people working in teams: Do the following exercises individually. Groups tend toward consensus. You don't want that yet. At this stage, you want diversity of language. This happens best individually. You will share your word lists with your other team members in Step 4.

Also, there is a key concept in Step 2 that you might not do often: free association. Free association is when you pick a starting place and let your mind wander. You go from word to word with little or no apparent connections. This is the backbone of a good brainstorm. You should not be able to explain the logic of how the list went from one word to the next. You are trusting your brain to make unconscious connections. It will do it if you give yourself the space. The main barrier to success with this concept is the fear of looking foolish. But remember—there are no wrong answers, so you can't really fail. There are examples later in this step of how I free-associate based on different starting points. But let's start by firming up your ideas.

MAKE IT CONCRETE

The first stage in your brainstorming process is to come up with five tangible sentences about your organization or product. For example, Bullhorn is a branding company. Here is what I would say about our company:

+ We design logos.
+ We write tag lines.
+ We build websites.
+ We make marketing materials.
+ We take photographs.

Here is the basic sentence diagram for the first bullet point: "We" is the subject, "design" is the verb, and "logos" is the object. Here are a few more sample sentences from other types of businesses:

+ We build schools.
+ We create financial plans.
+ We teach kids.
+ We clean commercial buildings.
+ We engineer hydration products.

As you can see, the subject/verb/object format creates simple, to-the-point, and effective statements about a business. Let's try it and see what you come up with in the exercises below. First start with some sentence generation, and then use those sentences to brainstorm more verbs and objects that could potentially become part of your company name. I've broken it up into three separate mini-exercises so you can see how they build on one another as you go.

MAKE IT CONCRETE BRAINSTORM

First, stop and write five sentences about your organization. It is important to use a different verb in each sentence.

1. _____

2. _____

3. _____

4. _____

5. _____

MAKE IT CONCRETE BRAINSTORM

Verb Brainstorm

Refer to your five sentences from the make it concrete exercise. Start with the verbs. (In the first sentence about Bullhorn, the verb is "design.") From there, start making a free-association list. Let your mind wander. There are no wrong answers here. The further out you go, the better.

I will start with my verb, "design," and list:

+ pencil

+ computer

+ Steve Jobs

+ intuition

+ paper

+ pixels

+ blueprints

+ lines

+ sketch

+ form

+ symbols

Note that there is no logical progression from word to word. You might be able to guess at the connections, but it is simply my brain looking at one word and suggesting another. Remember, you aren't trying to think of names at this point. You're just generating words. I am unlikely to name a company "Steve Jobs," but it's the word that came to mind when I saw the word "computer." You never know what an idea will lead to.

MAKE IT CONCRETE BRAINSTORM

We all have internal editors telling us that an idea is stupid or silly or too obvious. Shut that editor down! They have no business here.

Take the sentences you created in the make it concrete exercise. We're going to use them as the basis for this next brainstorm. Now make your lists of words based on the five verbs from your sentences. You should have 15 to 20 words for each verb you start with. Remember, the more diverse your lists are, the better. You will notice my list went from a concrete noun ("pencil") to a more abstract concept ("form").

1. _____

2. _____

3. _____

4. _____

5. _____

6. _____

7. _____

8. _____

9. _____

10. _____

11. _____

MAKE IT CONCRETE BRAINSTORM

12. _____

13. _____

14. _____

15. _____

Objects Brainstorm

Next we turn from verbs to objects. Remember my sentence: "We design logos." My starting point for the next brainstorm exercise would be the word "logos." Here is the objects list I created based on that one word:

+ shapes

+ companies

+ Paul Rand

+ IBM

+ Watson

+ cloud computing

+ lightning

+ summer

+ strawberries

+ picnic

From the list above you can see how Paul Rand (a famous logo designer) led me down an avenue pretty far from where I started. His

MAKE IT CONCRETE BRAINSTORM

name took me in turn to IBM and then Watson. (Rand designed the current IBM logo in 1972.)

From there, I went to cloud computing and summer storms. Again, I did this without really thinking about it. The thought of a cloud led me to a strong memory of a specific picnic. Unrelated, tangential words can be really evocative. You might be able to feel the heat of the sun, the condensation on the outside of a can, the rough fabric of the blanket. Maybe you can picture someone's smile. Allow yourself to go down these roads. Your memories are powerful. They are part of you. Why not make them a part of the brand you are creating, too?

You can always come back to the start if you get lost down a side road. Here is another free-associative list with a different starting point for the word "logos":

+ lines

+ signs

+ supermarkets

+ choice

+ color

+ packaging

+ die lines

+ printers

+ ink

This list is more in line with what the company does, but it's arguably less interesting. People are interesting. Businesses are made up of people. People buy your products or services. Don't be afraid to be interesting.

MAKE IT CONCRETE BRAINSTORM

Pick four objects from your make it concrete exercise. Create a list of 15 to 20 words for each object.

Object 1 _____

_____

_____

_____

_____

_____

_____

_____

_____

_____

_____

_____

_____

_____

_____

MAKE IT CONCRETE BRAINSTORM

_____

_____

_____

_____

_____

Object 2 _____

_____

_____

_____

_____

_____

_____

_____

_____

_____

_____

_____

MAKE IT CONCRETE BRAINSTORM

_____

_____

_____

_____

_____

_____

_____

_____

Object 3 _____

_____

_____

_____

_____

_____

_____

_____

Make It Concrete Brainstorm

_____

_____

_____

_____

_____

_____

_____

_____

_____

_____

Object 4 _____

_____

_____

_____

_____

_____

Make It Concrete Brainstorm

_____

_____

_____

_____

_____

_____

_____

_____

_____

_____

_____

_____

_____

MAKE IT ABSTRACT

It is a little hard to define what "abstract" means. For our purposes, it is a way of talking about something that isn't literally true but describes it in a way that exceeds what is possible with literal language. Ernest Hemingway wrote a short story called "Hills Like White Elephants." He could have called it "White Sand Hills" or "Snow-Capped Hills."

That might have been technically more accurate, but using the abstract image of the elephant makes it infinitely richer, and it sets up the story in a way a literal title could not.

Don't be intimidated. People speak in the abstract all the time. Figurative language (which you read about earlier) gives depth to the way we speak. Metaphors and similes are the primary tools for both figurative language (from Step 1) and abstract description (here in Step 2). For example, Bullhorn is a design/build firm. Technically, a design/build firm designs a building, makes the blueprints, and then builds it. Bullhorn doesn't do that, but there are some parallels between that and what Bullhorn does for brands. We do the research, create the brand strategy, and build out the brand.

It is also common to hear branding companies call themselves "storytellers." That isn't explicitly true—it's just a metaphor for how they help their clients communicate better. Or, at Bullhorn, we call ourselves "business therapists." Again, there are no licensed therapists on staff. But Bullhorn allows clients to talk about themselves and their businesses in a way that can often feel like a therapy session. It can certainly be cathartic.

Metaphors allow you to think about what you do in new and interesting ways. They help you apply something you know in a different context to your own. The above concepts of design/build, storytellers, and therapists all give us a richer sense of our job. They add dimensions we wouldn't have if we only thought of ourselves as designers and writers.

People use figurative, metaphorical language in their everyday lives, too. They are so common they often escape notice. It starts early. Think about children's songs: "You are my sunshine." They use metaphors to describe how they feel: *a little blue, under the weather, my heart is broken*. Metaphors describe actions: *I have been running around all day*. Probably not true unless you are training for a marathon.

A word of caution before you begin listing abstract metaphors for your business: like the above examples of feeling blue, or being under the weather, there are some metaphors that are so overused they have become clichés. Trees are a good example. They have roots. They endure over time. They provide shade and create oxygen for us to breathe. Many businesses, from banks to footwear manufacturers to plumbers, relate to one of these attributes. So do your research. Each industry will have overused names—and likely overused metaphors. Be strong like a tree and don't bend to the temptation of clichés. (See what I did there?)

Abstract Metaphors

Now stop to think about how you, your clients, or your customers talk about your business. What are three metaphors you or they use? Are you a magician, mixologist, or maestro? Are you a rock, road map, or religion? Here are a few examples of how brands use metaphors to convey abstract concepts about their businesses:

+ Red Bull Gives You Wings
+ Skittles: Taste the Rainbow
+ Budweiser: King of Beers

You can use three metaphors as a starting point for a list of word associations. Here is how I would go from an abstract metaphor to a concrete list of usable words. To do this, I am going back to the design/build metaphor for Bullhorn. I start by picturing an actual design/build office. I am thinking of the architects I know, as well as all the TV shows I have seen that portray architects or builders. I am thinking of the words "design" and "build" separately, and I am thinking about what they mean together. I am thinking about the complicated process that takes an idea, makes it into a drawing, and eventually produces a finished building. Here is my list:

+ blueprints

+ drafting table
+ ruler
+ hard hat
+ boots
+ hammer
+ nails
+ steel
+ dirt
+ backhoe
+ exhaust
+ noise

As you can see, this is a very different list than the one I would have come up with if I had started with the therapist metaphor. Let's try using that metaphor and see what words we come up with. This time, I start by picturing a therapist's office I am familiar with. I also pull from pop culture and combine all this to create a composite image in my mind:

+ couch
+ notepad
+ degrees
+ books
+ Sopranos
+ sanitation
+ mother
+ shrink
+ medication

Ultimately, you want to come up with lists of words that feel weird to you—that are unrelated to each other and to the core function of your business. Only then will you have the raw material (another metaphor) to create some interesting names that are rooted in abstract thinking. The lists should not be literal descriptions of what your business intends to do or already does.

Metaphors Exercise

If you are working in a small group, assign one person the task of gathering each member's lists and combining them into one document. It will be helpful to have as many words as possible when you move from generating words to making names. Have them omit any duplicate words.

Metaphors

To start, write down your three metaphors. What do people say about your company? How do you describe yourself internally? Remember: think in the abstract here.

1. _____

2. _____

3. _____

Similes

If you are stuck on metaphors, you might find similes easier. Think back to middle school grammar. A simile is a piece of figurative language that uses "like" or "as." This gives you a little more latitude in how you think of your business. What are three similes you can associate with your brand? Are you like a Viking ship? Are you like a cozy hammock? Are you like a westbound train?

+ State Farm: Like a good neighbor
+ Almond Joy/Mounds: Sometimes you feel like a nut; sometimes you don't.
+ Chevrolet: Like a rock

Write down three similes for your business. Just as with the metaphors, what do people say about you?

1. _____

2. _____

3. _____

METAPHOR BRAINSTORM

Now it's time to brainstorm again. Remember the concept of free association? We are going to list words associated with your metaphors and/or similes to generate more language. Create a list of 5-10 words based on each metaphor.

Metaphor 1

1. _____

2. _____

3. _____

4. _____

5. _____

6. _____

7. _____

8. _____

9. _____

10. _____

METAPHOR BRAINSTORM

Metaphor 2

1. _____

2. _____

3. _____

4. _____

5. _____

6. _____

7. _____

8. _____

9. _____

10. _____

Metaphor 3

1. _____

2. _____

3. _____

4. _____

5. _____

METAPHOR BRAINSTORM

6. _____

7. _____

8. _____

9. _____

10. _____

Simile 1

1. _____

2. _____

3. _____

4. _____

5. _____

6. _____

7. _____

8. _____

9. _____

10. _____

METAPHOR BRAINSTORM

Simile 2

1. _____
2. _____
3. _____
4. _____
5. _____
6. _____
7. _____
8. _____
9. _____
10. _____

Simile 3

1. _____
2. _____
3. _____
4. _____
5. _____

METAPHOR BRAINSTORM

6. _____

7. _____

8. _____

9. _____

10. _____

CASE STUDY
Caterpillar

Caterpillar is a truly bizarre name for a company that specializes in big equipment sales and service. Like many companies, Caterpillar was born out of an innovation in the marketplace. Tractors in the late 1800s were incredibly heavy, steam-powered behemoths.

The wheels would get buried in the earth, making them difficult to move. Caterpillar's bright idea was that a continuous track might be more effective than wheels. The newfangled machines the company created looked strange and unfamiliar. As the story goes, a company photographer remarked, "If that don't look like a monster caterpillar." The name stuck.

This story shows the utility of associations. Of course, the new tractor didn't *really* look like a caterpillar. But the motion of the track, and the way it crawled across the ground, reminded people of how caterpillars moved. Thus the association. In the

CASE STUDY, CONT.

brainstorming process, a literal description isn't necessary. Impressions are valuable.

But what else does the word "caterpillar" mean? *Caterpillar* is the larval stage of many insects. The main job of a caterpillar is to eat everything in its path in preparation for transformation. Caterpillars are often bad news for farmers. They can destroy crops and orchards with their voracity. The creatures—and by extension the word—are a prediction of devastation.

It is possible to go down a dark road thinking about what Caterpillar is devouring in this metaphor. The draft animals it replaces? The farmers it displaces? The earth itself? But that is only so useful. Let's not get carried away.

A caterpillar can just as easily be seen positively. It is also a state of possibility. It is potential. It may remind you of your favorite garden. You can't control what people think about your name. But it is a valuable habit to think about all the different ways it could be perceived.

What about the name's pronunciation? Technically, the *er* in the middle of the word is pronounced, giving it an unpleasant *er/er* repetition. However, the middle *er* is commonly dropped in favor of "cat-*a*-piller." All that is interesting, but ultimately it doesn't really matter.

Caterpillar is now referred to in shorthand as CAT. That is worth a second look, too. The construction equipment industry has historically been and is still dominated by men. The Bureau of Labor Statistics reports that as of 2018, only 3.4 percent of those who work in construction are women. It is primarily men

CASE STUDY, CONT.

making, selling, and operating these machines. Cats, however, have historically been associated with the feminine. They are characterized by graceful movement, certainly not an attribute of the clumsy, lumbering machines. So the shortening of the name is even more curious.

Why does it work, then? It works because it sounds great. And while the *meaning* of the word skews feminine, the word itself is the epitome of masculinity. It is curt. It is almost an exclamation. The hard *k* sound starts the word abruptly and propels it with great velocity through the soft *a* and toward the hard stop of the *t*. It is a jarring word. If you had to put the sound of a jackhammer into language, you might say it sounded like "cat-cat-cat-cat-cat."

So while an analysis of the name leaves us scratching our heads, it still ends up working very well. The tension between the word's meaning and the reality of the company just makes the name more interesting and, therefore, memorable.

STEP 2 TAKEAWAYS ⟶

Step 2 was more about setting up for the naming process than learning tons of new content. Your brain is probably feeling a little tired. These activities can be a strain until you get used to them. But good work making it this far. The work will pay off. Here is a summary of what we learned:

1. Brainstorming is important even though it is difficult because the only way to come up with a good name is to start with lots of options.

2. Brainstorming is easier when it's systematic. We started by making some concrete statements about your business and used them as jumping-off points for creating lists of words.

3. Try using more abstract language to facilitate your brainstorms. You can use metaphors and similes that speak to a facet of your business to create additional lists of words.

4. While Caterpillar is a very strange company name, it has some good things going for it. Think about how a similar approach might impact your naming conventions.

STEP 3

COMPILING NAMES

This is where you put all your brainstorming to the test by converting your ideas into actual names. Get your lists of words from Step 2 handy, because in this step we will use categories of names to generate a bank of possibilities. If you love making lists, this is where you can really shine.

One of the best ways to generate lists of possible names is to assign them to various categories that you can narrow down later. Some of these categories include foreign language words, compounds, and phrase names. Generating names in some categories will be much easier than in others. Stick with it, though. Each category represents a valid naming strategy, and it is best to have some options in each category. This is because without categories, you may tend to gravitate toward only one style of name. This exercise ensures you will have some diversity in name types to choose from.

The first category is real words. This is most people's default category and will likely be the easiest to fill. You know lots of real words, so naturally they come to mind first. One example is the luggage company Away. Your brainstorming lists will be a rich source of material for this section. But don't limit yourself to that. Inevitably, new words will come to mind as you work.

Real words are sometimes great conceptually, but too generic in practice. One way to get the full benefit of a real word is to translate it into a foreign language. Foreign language words is a rich category that works well for many types of businesses. And, no, you don't need to be fluent in multiple languages. We will go from your brainstorming lists to online language translators to build up a list of foreign language names to consider.

An additional way to use your real words as building blocks is to create compound names, our next category. Facebook is a good example. Both root words (face and book) are too generic to be a name on their own, but together they create something unique that is easy to say and remember and sounds great. Sometimes combining a common word you like with another word can make magic.

That said, a compound you like might be too long or complicated. I gave the example of PlantFactory in the introduction. You can use those awkward compounds to create blended names, the next category. These names work similarly to compound names. Instead of the words sitting next to each other (as in Facebook), they overlap. They share a syllable. For example, the end of "pin" can overlap with the beginning of "interest." Put them together, and you have a new word: Pinterest. This is a great blend because the word itself describes the core purpose of the platform. It exists so you can "pin" up things that interest you and show them to others.

When you were brainstorming, you may have unearthed some phrases. Those get their own category, too. Phrase names range from the ultra-generic, like the Bob's Car Wash example we mentioned earlier, to the more eccentric, like 7 For All Mankind.

The category that will require the most work is made-up names. You can start with words on your brainstorming lists, but it isn't a one-to-one relationship. These names require some tinkering. The good news is that you don't have to invent a new word from scratch. You can take words and start changing them until the end result is different enough to be unrecognizable. Can you imagine starting with Hype and changing things until you get to Skype? There are a couple of exercises that will give you the tools to try below.

The last category we will work with is people and place names. This category is pretty straightforward. These names are so common they can be a little bland. However, like anything else, with a little creativity you can use this category to your advantage. Start thinking about the people and places associated with your company.

As you work through Step 3, you will probably feel your internal editor creeping in, trying to chime in on the names you generate. Try to wait until the end of this step before judging which names you like better than others. When you get to Step 5, you will refer to the criteria you have established and make some judgments. Knowing that you can wait to judge will help you get past your preferences and get to something that works more strategically. Give yourself at least 20 minutes with each category.

At the end of this step, you will have 30 potential names.

REAL WORDS

Real-word names can work well for many types of businesses. They tend to be familiar and have associated meaning from the start. If you are starting a company and want it to feel established, this could be a good way to go. Because the words are familiar, your company will seem familiar, too.

But familiarity is also the downside of real-word names. Words that are too familiar will drift into the background because they are too common to be memorable. Also, if you wish to trademark your name, familiar words are often an issue. But not all real words are familiar. There are plenty of great, uncommon real words out there.

To get some real-word names on your list, go back to the lists of words you created in Step 2. Could any of them stand on their own as single-word names? Do any strike you as a little strange, but interesting? Do they catch your eye? Are there any obvious winners? Here are a few examples of real-word names to use as references:

+ Apple
+ Kindle
+ Oracle
+ Pandora
+ Puma
+ Twitter

Don't worry if the meaning of the word seems too vague to signify your business. Many real-word names will need a modifier until the company is large enough to be known by one word. For example, some of the most common real-word company names started out with modifiers: Apple Computer, Giant Bicycles, and Viking Range, for example. When they were founded, all of them needed an additional descriptor. Now they are all commonly referred to by a single, real-word name: Apple, Giant, and Viking. You have time to grow into your name, too.

Real Words Exercise

Flip back to the brainstorm exercises from Step 2. Given all you have learned, which words could be names? Don't think too much about your criteria. Just look for something interesting. Here is one of my sample lists:

+ blueprints
+ drafting table
+ ruler
+ hard hat
+ boots
+ hammer
+ nails
+ steel
+ dirt
+ backhoe
+ exhaust
+ noise

If I were naming a branding company from this list, I would pull out "hard hat." I think that has some potential. I would also pull out "backhoe" because I like the alliteration with "branding." At this point I have no idea if they meet my criteria or if there are a thousand other companies by those names, but that doesn't matter right now. Dig into your lists and choose 5 to 10 words that stand out as possible names here.

1. _____

2. _____

3. _____

4. _____

5. _____

6. _____

7. _____

8. _____

9. _____

10. _____

FOREIGN LANGUAGE WORDS

You may wonder why you should consider words in a foreign language when English is hard enough to deal with. But there is a sea of beautiful language out there that you should explore. If your business is in a predominantly English-speaking country, a foreign name can help you stand out from your competition. You can sound different in a way that is either approachable or exclusive. Consider the difference between the example I used earlier—Yves Saint Laurent—and a name like Bonjour. One sounds serious and exclusive while the other seems fun and approachable.

Another reason to consider incorporating a foreign language word in your name is that it allows you to add meaning and nuance while still being literal. For example, if you own a restaurant famous for its salsa, Rojo might be a good name. It feels tangible and earthy without being overly literal or abstract. It is a nice middle path.

Or you might choose a foreign language word if you intend to do business both in the U.S. and internationally. If you have customers or suppliers in South or Central America, a Latin or Latin-based word might be a good idea. Spanish and Portuguese both descend from Latin, so Latinate words are more likely to feel natural, while English is mostly a mix of Latin and German heritage. So most Latin-based words work here, too.

Start your search with English words that you like but that are too commonly used, have a broad meaning, or are a cliché in your industry. For example, "money" is too general to be used as a name in any industry. But in French, it is *argent*. Or in Icelandic, it is *peninga*. Those are certainly more distinctive than "money." Try translating your words into Latin and then go to other Latinate languages like Spanish, French, and Italian.

Maybe you have Persian grandparents. Start there. While foreign language words can transform common words, they are even better if used purposefully. The choice of language could speak to you or your culture. The choice could speak to the product or the intended customers. This is common for food brands. For example, there is the Italian restaurant chain Buca di Beppo. I happen to know that it means "Joe's Basement," a reference to their origin in Minneapolis. But you don't have to know what it means to see that the name is fun to say and that it sounds Italian. Here are a few additional examples of foreign language names:

+ Corona
+ Verde
+ Rojo
+ Chiba
+ Avesta

A common concern with foreign words is that they will either be too hard to spell or too hard to pronounce. That is a legitimate worry. But it can be overcome. There are words in most languages that can feel familiar to English speakers. When looking through translations, you are looking for common letter combinations. You are looking for words that could be English, but aren't. Here are a few examples of foreign language names that follow English pronunciation patterns:

+ Honda
+ Toyota
+ Stoli
+ Peroni
+ Mercedes

Those are all words from across the world—from Japan to Russia to Italy to Germany—that are fairly easy for English speakers to spell and say. El Camino is one of my favorite brand names—it is easy to spell and gratifying to say even for the most challenged Spanish speaker. Plus, who doesn't like a car with a truck bed?

Foreign Language Words Exercise

It's time to find some foreign language words that might work as a name for your business. Start by using an online language translator. This allows for quick toggling between languages. Begin with your real word list from the previous exercise. Be broad in what you include here. There will be time to eliminate words later. You can flip back to the brainstorming word lists from Step 2 if you need more raw material. Compile a list of at least ten foreign language words based on English words from your existing lists.

1. _____

2. _____

3. _____

4. _____

5. _____

6. _____

7. _____

8. _____

9. _____

10. _____

COMPOUND WORDS

Using compound words is a great way to create a meaningful, approachable name. This is a good opportunity to use some of the words you might have also used as a starting point in the foreign language exercise: words that are too common, too broad, or a cliché in your industry. Compound names can take those kinds of words and assign them a more nuanced meaning. Often a good URL will be available—especially if you are pairing two words that aren't commonly joined together. And you can create words that are easier to trademark.

The goal of this section is to combine two common words to make something new. However, there are still rules—a recipe, you might say. For example, some words work better as the first half of a compound, while some work better as the second. Good first words end in soft consonants, like *f*, *s*, *l*, *r*, or *m*. That soft sound makes it easier to transition to the second word. Good second words end solidly, with a strong consonant, like *k*, *x*, *t*, or *d*. They are gratifying to say and don't linger, like words that end with *s* or *l*. Here are a few compound names. Some adhere to the rule above. Some don't. Take a look:

+ Facebook
+ Firefox
+ Salesforce
+ WordPress
+ YouTube

The main thing you want is a smooth transition between the words. WordPress is the outlier here, but it still works because your mouth naturally transitions from the *d* sound at the end of "word" to the *p* sound at the beginning of "press." That smooth transition is vital because you are trying to create a whole word out of two parts. You want the compound to feel seamless, as if it had always existed. Again, Facebook is a good example of this. Even though the two original words are common, the new name feels complete and natural.

Salesforce is an interesting example. The second *s* in "sales" sustains until you start pronouncing the *f*. No matter how long you take to start saying "force," the *s* sound creates a bridge that unites the words. While it doesn't end with a hard consonant, it still works really well. The sound of the soft *c* at the end of the second word brings you back to the two *s* sounds in the first word, reinforcing that the name is a cohesive whole.

Firefox and YouTube have a similar bridge-like transition. The *r* in "fire" resonates until you transition to the *f* sound. The same thing happens with the *u* sound in "you." Both first words end in a way that provides unity and cohesion to the names. The second words both end with strong consonants that give a sense of resolution to the names.

Here is a made-up example. Take two arbitrarily chosen words: say, "laugh" and "act." When combined, notice that the order matters. "Actlaugh" is unsatisfying to say. The *t* in the middle makes you stop and restart the word unpleasantly. And the *f* sound at the end doesn't provide much resolution. If you switch the order, it is much improved: Laughact. Now the *f* sound transitions nicely into the *a*, making it more fluid. The *ct* at the end provides a clearer finish, giving it a more solid feel. It's undoubtedly still a weird word. But hopefully the point is clear: Some words work better in the front, and some at the end. Spend some time sitting with each compound word you come up with and saying it out loud. What do you hear?

Compound Words Exercise

Look at your brainstorming lists. Choose two lists and sort the words into two categories: front-half words and second-half words.

Front half

1. _____

2. _____

3. _____

4. _____

5. _____

6. _____

7. _____

8. _____

9. _____

10. _____

Second half

1. _____

2. _____

3. _____

4. _____

5. _____

6. _____

7. _____

8. _____

9. _____

10. _____

Now, using these two lists, create ten compound names. Some of these words will work better than others. Don't hesitate to use a word more than once.

1. _____

2. _____

3. _____

4. _____

5. _____

6. _____

7. _____

8. _____

9. _____

10. _____

PHRASES

Phrases are common in local business names: Bob's Car Wash, Safety First Day Care, etc. But if you were going to use a straightforward descriptive name like that, you probably wouldn't have picked up this book. Phrase names work best if they are surprising or provide insight into the brand. A phrase can also provide a great hook to start telling your brand's story.

You will notice phrase names are similar to compound names. There are generally two ways they are different. One, they tend to have a space between the words. And two, the words usually work as a phrase to say something sensible. While you kind of get what "Facebook" means, it isn't a common phrase construction.

When creating a phrase name, there are still some rules to follow. One common construction is to combine a modifier with a noun:

+ Black Diamond
+ Home Depot
+ Green Thumb
+ Mountain Dew

There are also some longer phrase names. Sometimes these are observations about the product:

+ Dave's Killer Bread
+ I Can't Believe It's Not Butter

Sometimes the name can be a common phrase or a play on a common phrase:

+ Fruit of the Loom
+ Bon Appetit

Speaking of Fruit of the Loom, is the name a play on "fruit of the vine," meaning "the loom bears fruit," which is something useful? Or is it a play on the phrase "fruit of your loins"? I mean, it *is* selling underwear. Pretty risqué for a company that is nearly 170 years old, right? Unfortunately, that isn't the real story. In reality, the name came from an interesting observation. Initially, the B.B. and R. Knight Corporation produced and sold high-quality cotton fabrics. When visiting a customer, Mr. Knight asked why some of the bolts of fabric had apples painted on them. It turns out his customer's daughter painted them, and the painted bolts sold better. Mr. Knight saw the apple as the perfect symbol for the company and changed the name to Fruit of the Loom. Fruit for the apple and loom for the machinery producing the cloth.

Phrases Exercise

There might already be some short phrases in your list of words. Look at those. Also look for single words that prompt phrases. What does the word "hammer" make you think of? Hammer and Nail? Hammer Time? Ten-Pound Hammer? Try creating multiple phrase names from a single word. Using your brainstorming lists as a starting point, create 10 phrase names that move beyond a surface description.

1. _____

2. _____

3. _____

4. _____

5. _____

6. _____

7. _____

8. _____

9. _____

10. _____

BLENDED WORDS

A blended word is a new word that is composed of two parts. It is similar to a compound word in the sense that you are creating a new word out of component parts, but the result is quite a bit different. The end name looks less familiar and stands out from the start. Here are some examples that were once very strange, but seem obvious and familiar now:

+ Group + coupon = Groupon
+ Pin + interest = Pinterest
+ Unique + clothing = Uniqlo
+ Microcomputer + software = Microsoft
+ Accent + future = Accenture

In the examples above, what makes Groupon easier to say than Uniqlo? When creating these words, there is one very important rule to follow: Avoid something called *awkwordplay*[1]. The term describes a common mistake namers make when creating blended words. The idea was coined by Christopher Johnson, the author of *Microstyle* and creator of The Name Inspector blog. The term itself is an example of a common problem with blended words. It isn't clear which syllable to emphasize. The first syllable of "awkward" and the first syllable of "wordplay" should both be emphasized. When they are blended into "awkwordplay," you don't know which syllable to stress, the first or the second. It sounds weird either way.

So be clear which syllable is emphasized. Groupon follows this rule and is easy to pronounce, as is Pinterest. Uniqlo doesn't do this, and the pronunciation is ambiguous. The second syllable of "unique" and the first syllable of "clothing" are emphasized. When they are blended, it isn't clear if the second or third syllable of "Uniqlo" should be emphasized. Because of that, the word feels awkward.

Blended Words Exercise

A good starting place for creating blended words is to take some of the phrases or compounds from the previous two exercises. Try smooshing a few words together by eliminating a syllable of one word. (You would be right to note that "smooshing" isn't a very technical term. But I like it, and, hey, it's kind of a blend itself.) Again, refer to your brainstorming lists if you need more words. Try to create 10 new blended words here:

1. _____

2. _____

3. _____

4. _____

5. _____

6. _____

7. _____

8. _____

9. _____

10. _____

MADE-UP WORDS

So far you have learned about two types of names you can create out of spare parts: compound and blended words. Compound words are still recognizable as names made of two words. Blended words go a step further. They are sometimes recognizable, but not always. Now we will go one step past that. We are going to create some words that don't have any clear trace of their origins.

There is a French term called *bricolage*. It roughly translates as "to tinker" or "DIY." In art, it means that everything we create contains bits of other things. Picasso contains bits of Cezanne who contains bits of Pissarro. It may be that there aren't truly made-up words, but that they are cleverly disguised pieces of bricolage.

The main reason to create a brand name in this way is because you feel strongly that your company should have a unique name. It's a bold way to go. Feeling bold? Here are a few ways to start creating new words.

Vowel Substitution

Pick some words from your brainstorming lists. If you are starting to wear out those lists, try making a few more using the techniques from Step 2. You can start changing the words by swapping out vowels. I picked the word "small" from my list. "Smoll" and "smull" don't look or sound particularly attractive. "Smill" is interesting, though. While I was positive I had just made up this word, it turns out it already exists on the internet and has some meanings I might not want associated with my company. So I'll move on to other options.

Consonant Substitution

You can also try swapping consonants, though this is sometimes harder. Continuing with the "small" example, spall and stall are already real words. Sdall and Sball look like mistakes. Scall and skall are strange-looking and sound like "skull." What about smahh or smaff? This is a tricky method, but it can be worth it if you can get past the weird words you may produce along the way.

Onomatopoeia

We discussed this concept in the memorability section in Step 1. *Onomatopoeia* is when a word is spelled the way it sounds: Meow, chirp, roar, and tick-tock are all examples. Try writing out the sounds of things you hear. For example, if you like owls, try spelling the sound they make as you hear it. It probably won't be "hoot," although that is an onomatopoeia, too.

Here are a few made-up names:

+ Bebo
+ Etsy

+ Lexus
+ Häagen-Dazs

When making up words, there is one good test you can use to determine if the word is likely to work well: the rhyme test. Is there a real word that rhymes with your made-up word? If so, it is more likely the name will be adopted. That means the name has a common construction even if the letter combination is unique. You will notice there are rhyming words for each of the names in the list above: placebo, Betsy, Texas. OK, there isn't really anything that rhymes with Häagen-Dazs. That's because the founder wasn't trying to create a word that sounded English. He wanted something that sounded Danish and that would position them alongside European confectioners.

When you make up a word, you are choosing a name that doesn't have a literal meaning. But you will have a significant advantage if it *feels* like a real word. Hold your names up to the rhyme test.

Made-Up Words Exercise

Pull ten words from your brainstorming lists. Use the methods outlined in this section to create ten brand-new, made-up names.

1. _____

2. _____

3. _____

4. _____

5. _____

6. _____

7. _____

8. _____

9. _____

10. _____

PEOPLE AND PLACE NAMES

Names derived from proper nouns are also real words, but they get their own category because generating them requires more focused efforts. You may not be able to generate many place names off the top of your head. That is OK. In Step 4, you will learn how to use some research methods to expand this list.

There are several reasons you might want to use names derived from people or places. One is to reference people or places that add meaning to your name. LA Fitness is a good example. Los Angeles is known as a place where people stay in shape. I live in Kentucky, which generally ranks last or second-to-last in fitness. Calling your gym KY Fitness wouldn't seem very impressive. However, Kentucky has historically been known for growing tobacco and for high rates of smoking. So Kentucky's Best would make sense as a brand of cigarettes. Conversely, LA's Best doesn't really ring true as a cigarette brand. If you are interested, 23 percent of Kentucky adults smoke compared to 11 percent in Los Angeles.

Or take Doubleday & Cartwright, a creative agency that focuses on the sports industry. They get their name from Abner Doubleday and Alexander Cartwright, two founders of modern baseball. The company feels established right off the bat thanks to those names. They also chose to combine two innovators of the sport. That makes the name feel more professional than if it were a single first-and-last-name construction.

Franklin Templeton Investments is an investment management company. It was named after founding father Ben Franklin, who was famous for advising frugality and once wrote, "Rather go to bed supperless than rise in debt." ("Templeton" comes from a later merger.) Ben Franklin is a great mascot for a company helping people invest for the future.

Look at this list of examples. Can you guess the rationale behind the names?

+ Patagonia
+ California Pizza Kitchen
+ Samsonite
+ Tesla

Let's unpack these. Patagonia is (or at least was) an exotic destination in Argentina. The mountainous region is a great name for a company making clothing for whatever outdoor adventure you undertake. California Pizza Kitchen makes high-quality pizza with nontraditional toppings, such as barbecue chicken, Thai chicken, and shrimp scampi. California is known for reinvention, and CPK is the reinvention of pizza. Samsonite creates luggage strong enough for Samson himself. And then there's Tesla. Nikola Tesla was an inventor, a mechanical engineer, and an electrical engineer. He was prolific. His work in electrical motors and alternating current paved the way for current electrical cars making him a perfect namesake for the company.

People and Place Names Exercise

To start, look back at your brainstorming lists. Did any people, places, or things come to mind during the exercises in Step 2? If you look back at my sample lists, three names came up: the Watson computer, Paul Rand, and Steve Jobs. I did not plan for that. It just happened. List any people or places you came up with below.

1. _____

2. _____

3. _____

4. _____

5. _____

Now list five additional places you would like to have associated with your business.

1. _____

2. _____

3. _____

4. _____

5. _____

List five people notable in your industry.

1. _____

2. _____

3. _____

4. _____

5. _____

List a notable person for each metaphor on page 58.

1. _____

2. _____

3. _____

4. _____

5. _____

List a notable person for each simile on page 60.

1. _____

2. _____

3. _____

4. _____

5. _____

Now, out of all those places and names, list five that might make a good brand name for you:

1. _____

2. _____

3. _____

4. _____

5. _____

ADDITIONAL TYPES OF NAMES

There are three other common types of names not included in the above categories: initialisms/acronyms, affixed, and misspellings.

There is nothing wrong with these names, but there are reasons they don't make sense in this exercise. Acronyms are usually chosen because they are the lesser of two evils when compared with a long, unwieldy name. But that doesn't mean they're good. You wouldn't choose a pile of initials from the beginning if you took the time to think about it, which you are.

Affixed names (a word with an added letter or syllable at the beginning or end) and misspellings are trendy, but the pitfalls mentioned below usually outweigh the potential benefits. That said, these three types of names deserve some attention because they are very common these days. In some industries, they are the norm. For example, if you are trying to name a trade association, 99 percent of your competitors have an acronym as a name. It will be tempting to do the same and make the safe choice. Resist. You can do better. Let's take a deeper look at these types of names.

Initialisms and Acronyms

Most people confuse these (including me), so I combined them into one section, although they are actually two different things. An *initialism* is made of letters you pronounce independently (like "FBI"). An *acronym* is an abbreviation you say like a word (like "NASA"). Generally, you opt for one of these after choosing an overly long name or going through a significant change in the business so that the original name is no longer accurate. If you are working on the front edge of artificial intelligence and your name is International Business Machines, you shorten it to IBM. If your name is Minnesota Mining and Manufacturing and now you make your money from sandpaper and Post-it notes, you might settle for 3M.

It is worth noting that 3M is a better name than Minnesota Mining and Minerals. It is also better than MMM. But if the company were starting up today, 3M would be an odd choice.

The issue is that initialisms are forgettable and pretty boring. They are a fallback plan. Acronyms can be better. Sometimes they even fit in the made-up word category, but I didn't want to muddy the waters for you. Take Geico, which is actually the Government Employees Insurance Company. Taser is really a loose acronym taken from an old children's book, *Tom Swift and His Electric Rifle*. But few people realize it—they just sound like weird or made-up words. And when it comes to names, weird is often good.

Affixed

Affixed names are frequently identified with internet companies. The formula is pretty straightforward. Take a real word, and either put something in front of it, like the *i* in iPhone, or put something at the end, like the *ster* in Napster. These sorts of names can yield some interesting results, but they are easily copied. And, even if you are the first for a naming convention, you can still be made generic by all of the fast followers. Spotify was founded in 2006. It wasn't the first company to use a name ending in *ify*. But its founders probably couldn't have predicted the hundreds of companies that would follow in the wake of its success, including Crowdify, Couponify, Userify, and Playlistify. At this point, the *ify* naming structure is a joke that Spotify probably does not think is funny. Affixed names tend to be trendy, which makes it hard to separate yourself from current and potential competition.

Misspellings

Misspellings (the intentional kind) can occasionally work, but there are serious pitfalls. For one, they can look a little amateurish. Local businesses are a rich source of tacky misspellings, like "korner," "kuts," and "pawz," which will now stick out at you like terribly hammered thumbs.

These are also associated with internet companies. URL scarcity was a main driver of this phenomenon. Now that there are more domain extensions available, it is less of an issue, including .com, .net, .io, .it, .biz, .ly, and so on.

There is some research, as we mentioned in Step 1, that indicates that for new or relatively unknown names, misspellings can make them more memorable. There are, of course, successful companies with misspelled names:

+ La-Z-Boy
+ Krispy Kreme
+ Chick-fil-A
+ Kraft
+ Publix

Now, I support any naming strategy that works. Clearly these types of names have worked to some degree, or the companies would not be as successful as they are. La-Z-Boy sounds like a product from the 1920s (which it was; the company was founded in 1928). There is a sense of nostalgia about the name that makes it work. It was a time of new products for people with disposable income. Almost certainly one of your grandparents owned one of their chairs. But you have to draw the line somewhere, and the others are pretty hard to defend. Publix and Krispy Kreme are especially terrible to look at.

The bottom line is that people do use deliberately misspelled brand names, but you shouldn't unless you have a really good reason. And even then you probably still shouldn't. The disadvantages generally outweigh any points you earn for uniqueness.

CASE STUDY
Viagra

One of the most successful naming exercises of the late 20th century is Viagra. Erectile dysfunction is embarrassing. And it isn't just about sex. The lack of potency is a reminder that our bodies are aging. Your business or product might face some challenges, but likely none as formidable as those associated with Viagra.

CASE STUDY, CONT.

It's said that when the naming team was doing research for the project, they met with patients in the clinical trials. When asked what taking the medication felt like, one of the patients said that they felt like a force of nature.[2] From there, they combined the two common words "vigorous" and "Niagara." I don't at all believe this story is true. It is too convenient. But, it is useful. Niagara is one of the first images that comes to mind when we hear the word Viagra. The waterfall is powerful. It is loud.

The next thing to consider is how the word is constructed. The prefix *via* commonly refers to a path or road, which are frequently used as metaphors for life. We might see the *vi* and think of "vitality" or "vigor." The suffix *agra* refers to pain, but that is a clinical term and not commonly known. We usually think of the prefix *agri*, which relates to agriculture, or to fertility and virility (another *vi* word). Or we might hear the *agr* and think of "aggression." Regardless, the new word was a smashing success. It took parts of familiar words and made something new.

The icing on the cake is that Viagra sounds like the Sanskrit word for tiger (vyahgrah). Who doesn't want to be a sex tiger?

Viagra is easy to spell and sounds great. A good name can overcome significant barriers.

STEP 3 TAKEAWAYS ⟶

The main work of Step 3 was taking the lists of words from Step 2 and forming them into names. At this point, you aren't judging the names; you are simply creating them. As you have learned, the more you create, the better the end result will be. Here are some parting thoughts from Step 3:

1. We focused on seven primary name types: real words, foreign language words, compound words, phrases, blended words, made-up words, and people and place names.

2. We also looked briefly at three additional types of names: initialisms and acronyms, affixed words, and misspelled words. For various reasons, these types of names aren't very useful in these exercises.

3. Viagra is a great name on multiple fronts. It brings down some of the barriers that would keep a person suffering with erectile dysfunction from seeking treatment. Plus, it means "tiger" in Sanskrit.

STEP 4

EXPANDING
YOUR KNOWLEDGE

You have now worked through three steps of the naming process. You have established your criteria. You have created several brainstorming lists of words. And you have used those lists to create seven different types of possible names: real words, foreign language words, compound words, phrases, blended words, and made-up words. The effort so far has been primarily focused on getting what is in your head out and onto paper.

We are now going to change directions. You can put down your pen and paper and move to the computer, because it's time to do some research. It is difficult to apply a structured methodology to internet research. Research online can be like wandering around a foreign city without a map. Part of the fun is the aimless sense of discovery.

What follows is a set of five different starting points for your research—or your exploration, if you prefer. Follow these searches down as many random alleys as possible. Get off at unknown subway stops. That is where you will often find the most interesting ideas.

That said, there is one glaring issue with internet research. Even before this book is published, a new website or tool will come out that makes one of my suggestions irrelevant. Websites come and go quickly, and our ways of interacting with information change. What I hope to do here is give you flexible starting points that you can adapt as the world changes. Therefore, I won't be recommending a favorite online thesaurus or translation tool because I want this step to be relevant and useful for as long as possible.

Start by looking at a couple of online (or print) thesauruses (or thesauri, if you prefer the Latin plural). This will allow you to rapidly expand your vocabulary. You will use your brainstorming lists as a starting point, but quickly depart from them as you start to make interesting connections.

Next go to Wikipedia. This is a great tool for namers (although I don't recommend it for formal research). User-generated content grows very rapidly and boasts many interconnections. However, it is not authoritative. Information you uncover here will be a valuable signpost, but you will need to confirm its truthfulness elsewhere.

Literature is the third starting point. We will talk about quotations, favorite books, and other texts that are relevant to your business. We will also look at other businesses that have found names in famous books. Literature is a rich source of inspiration.

Next we will dig into insider lingo This is a rich mine of language. Every industry, sport, and hobby has its own vocabulary that defines insiders and outsiders. This is a good way to find real words that are obscure enough for you to trademark. It can also be a great starting place for a story of why you chose this strange word for your name.

The last jumping-off point is mythology. Every culture has at least one, but many of them are not well-known. Similar to insider lingo,

96 STEP 4: EXPANDING YOUR KNOWLEDGE

this is a good source of obscure real words, all of them with stories to tell.

Where the brainstorming step focused on what was already in your head, this step focuses on expanding your field of knowledge. By the time you finish working through the following five sections, you will have 30 more possible names to add to your list.

THESAURUS

Crack open a thesaurus. Any brand is fine—an online source or a printed book. Refer back to the words on your brainstorming lists, and in the synonyms for those words, look for interesting words related to your concepts. Go to the entry for one of the synonyms that looks promising, look at the words listed there, and repeat the process. Often the further you get from your starting point, the further the words get from being synonymous. That can be good. You are looking for loose relations rather than exact matches. You don't need to know what the words mean at this point. Just write them down and go from one word to the next. I went back to my sample lists from Step 2 and chose "hard hat." Here are some words from the thesaurus that stood out to me:

+ gabardine
+ balaclava
+ castanet
+ deerstalker
+ tinfoil

Are any of these words directly related to "hard hat"? Not really. They aren't even very close. Are they great names for a design agency? Maybe. It depends on my criteria list, which we established in Step 1. But none of them would have come to mind without a thesaurus.

So why did these words stand out to me? For one, the first four balance on that line of being familiar enough to be pronounceable without being so common that you pass over them unnoticed. The last one is common but is so out of context when I think of my company that I kept it. Another reason these words stand out is that I like saying them—especially the first three. I kept "deerstalker" because of the double entendre. I happened to know it is a type of hat, but it also has the descriptive meaning, which is interestingly out of context for a design agency.

There is a design agency called Mother. That name is so weird. It is one of the most common words in English, but it is so out of context that it works really well. It is both familiar and a little formal. Tinfoil might work the same way.

With the thesaurus exercise below, you are looking for interesting words tangential to the words on your brainstorming lists. Remember, they don't have to be directly related to the original word or to your business. The word can feel a little counterintuitive or uncommon.

Thesaurus Exercise

Starting with your brainstorming lists, write ten new words from a thesaurus. Don't overly edit. If you have more than ten, great. Go for it!

1. _____

2. _____

3. _____

4. _____

5. _____

6. _____

7. _____

8. _____

9. _____

10. _____

ENCYCLOPEDIA SOURCE LIKE WIKIPEDIA

Wikipedia is vast and wonderful, as are other, lesser-known wikis. The hyperlinked articles about concepts, people, and places make it easy to wander for much longer than you probably want to. You can really fall down the research rabbit hole. But keep in mind as you explore that it is a starting point. Any concept you uncover here you will need to cross-reference with a more established source to ensure you have your facts straight. The question is, where to start?

Think back to Step 2. How did you describe your business? For example, one of the words I use for Bullhorn is "storytelling." I typed "storytelling" into the Wikipedia search field. One of the hyperlinked terms was "oral storytelling." I clicked on that. On that page, I found the following words that would work as possible names:

+ vyasa
+ grimm
+ minstrel
+ bard
+ ozan

Now those are interesting words. They are recognizable, but they aren't words I would normally say in everyday life. Again, I probably wouldn't have thought of any of them when naming a design agency— or anything else. That is the beauty of research. These words are unexpected. And that is cool. That is also after only scratching the surface. I only clicked once. Imagine what you'll find if you go deep.

Wikipedia Exercise

Again, start with your brainstorming lists. The more abstract list might be the best starting point here because it could take you down some rather unconventional rabbit holes. Below, write ten new words from a Wikipedia article or topic based on that list. When you're done, try the same exercise using one of your other brainstorming lists.

1. _____

2. _____

3. _____

4. _____

5. _____

6. _____

7. _____

8. _____

9. _____

10. _____

LITERARY NAMES

Quotations are a great source of interesting names. There is a long tradition of books taking their titles from previous works. John Steinbeck took the name of his novel *The Grapes of Wrath* from the song "The Battle Hymn of the Republic." It is a good name that fits the book, but the choice of name was also strategic. The use of the patriotic lyric was an attempt to moderate the content of the book. Anti-communist sentiment was high in the United States at that time, and Steinbeck was a socialist. In fact, the first edition contained the sheet music and lyrics of the song on the inside cover. It didn't work.

The book was banned and burned in several counties when it was released in 1939. That's quite a back story. Does your business have similar cultural touchstones that can serve as inspiration for a new name?

What sources might provide a name to you? There are two sources that are far and away the most common in the western tradition. One is the Bible. Here are some examples:

+ *The Sun Also Rises*, Ernest Hemingway (Ecclesiastes 1:5)
+ *The Violent Bear It Away*, Flannery O'Connor (Matthew 11:12)
+ *East of Eden,* John Steinbeck (Genesis 4:16)
+ *Song of Solomon*, Toni Morrison (Song of Solomon)

And the works of Shakespeare:

+ *Brave New World*, Aldous Huxley (*The Tempest*)
+ *Something Wicked This Way Comes*, Ray Bradbury (*Macbeth*)
+ *The Sound and the Fury*, William Faulkner (*Macbeth*)
+ *Twice-Told Tales,* Nathaniel Hawthorne (*King John*)
+ *Infinite Jest*, David Foster Wallace (*Hamlet*)

If it's good enough for the most significant literature of the past two centuries, it's good enough for you. Look at your favorite play, verse, prayer, or meditation. Words that are meaningful to you add meaning to your business. And you don't have to limit yourself to western traditions. Plenty of companies like Prana have found inspiration in other literary or religious traditions, such as yoga.

Here are a few businesses with names taken from literary sources:

+ Yahoo! (*Gulliver's Travels*, Jonathan Swift)
+ Morningstar (*Walden*, Henry David Thoreau)
+ Starbucks (*Moby Dick*, Herman Melville)

Yahoo! is an interesting choice. In *Gulliver's Travels,* Swift takes his title character to many strange lands, including the island of the Houyhnhnms, a race of intelligent horses. Of all the peoples in the book, Swift treats them the most respectfully. Also living on the island is a group of unevolved humans, known as the Yahoos. The author describes them as "the most filthy, noisome, and deformed animals which nature ever produced . . . " They are "restive and indocible, mischievous and malicious." The founders of Yahoo! chose the name to be self-deprecating. It certainly is.

Literary Names Exercise

Write down your five favorite books. What words from the title or a significant quotation could function as a name?

1. _____

2. _____

3. _____

4. _____

5. _____

INSIDER LINGO

Every topic has its own vocabulary. These obscure words are a rich source for namers. One way to discover these words is to search for "list of _____ terms." Here are a few actual searches I have done for naming projects:

+ List of nautical terms
+ List of evergreen trees in the southern United States
+ List of Persian religious terms

You are looking for something that is uncommon enough to be a unique name. For example, if your business helps your clients navigate their health-care options, look for lists of terms related to navigation or orienteering. The best word is likely to be both uncommon and connected to your metaphor. You are setting up a story that you can tell again and again. The story should be short and say something about who you are and what kind of business you run.

However, there are so many lists on the internet it can be overwhelming. You will have to find a way to limit your search. There are lists of authors, battles, books, kites, wildflowers, smoked meats, timepieces, summer songs, coffees, teas, beers, whiskeys, and waters. There are lists for everything, and all of them are full of interesting and unusual words. Your metaphors may provide a good starting point, but it also might be helpful to search for lists of words relating to interesting topics. What are you passionate about? Gems? Microphones? Famous photographs?

For example, if you searched for lists of animals, you would get some pretty common words:

+ Puma
+ Jaguar
+ Crocodile (Crocs)
+ Dove
+ Camel

Those are all great brands, but those names are too common now. If you dig deeper into animals, you might find Reebok in a list of African antelopes, or The Famous Grouse in a list of Scottish moorland birds.

So as you dig into this exercise, get specific. Most of the general names are long gone. You want something you have likely never heard of before. However, keep an eye out for general ease of spelling and pronounceability as you are looking. Are there ways the word could be mispronounced? If so, is that OK with you?

Insider Lingo Exercise

Start with your metaphor brainstorming lists in Step 2. Each of those metaphors will have insider lingo associated with it. From there, move on to your wider lists. You should be able to find lists related to some of those words online. It can be as simple as types of hammers or writing utensils, for example. Based on this research, write down 10 words that might work as possible names.

1. _____

2. _____

3. _____

4. _____

5. _____

6. _____

7. _____

8. _____

9. _____

10. _____

MYTHOLOGY

Mythology is a great place to find interesting names with built-in meaning. Each culture has its own myths; in the U.S., Greek and Roman mythology is generally the most familiar. For example, if you are naming a construction company, you might look for builders in ancient Greek mythology. Hephaestus was the blacksmith of the gods, who built their homes, their furniture, their armor, and even their jewelry. But "Hephaestus" is hard to spell and pronounce. You need to look one level deeper. Since Greek gods usually had Roman counterparts, Hephaestus was called "Vulcan" in Roman mythology. That would be a great name for a construction company. Wait—it already is. In fact, several construction companies have used that name.

Here are a few more companies that got their names from mythology:

+ Aeron
+ Tyr
+ Oracle
+ Osiris
+ Venus

Aeron, the innovative chair created by the company, Herman Miller, is the name of a Welsh deity. Tyr is a global swimwear brand and also the Norse god of warriors. The name hints at the competitive culture of the sporting goods company.

There were several oracles in ancient times; the most famous is the Oracle of Delphi. They were places you would visit to get information about the future. That is a cool name if you are in at the dawn of the computing industry.

Osiris is a skate boarding shoe company. Osiris is also an Egyptian deity who judges the dead. The name literally means "powerful or mighty." Venus (Greek counterpart Aphrodite) is the Roman goddess associated with love, beauty, and fertility, which is a great name if you are starting a line of razors aimed at women.

Mythology Exercise

Now dig into your own mythological names. Again, start with your brainstorming list of metaphors. When something catches your eye, dig one step deeper. Write down 10 words from your mythology research.

1. _____

2. _____

3. _____

4. _____

5. _____

6. _____

7. _____

8. _____

9. _____

10. _____

EVEN GOOD COMPANIES CAN HAVE BAD NAMES

By this point, you are probably starting to feel a little stressed. I have good news for you. There are good companies with pretty bad names. That doesn't mean you can stop here and just choose something. A good name is an advantage you should give yourself. But it doesn't have to be the name to end all names. In fact, there are some really great companies out there that happen to have not-great names but are wildly successful anyway. Let's dig into a few reasons why a name might not work as well as you might think.

Problems with Pronunciation

Most companies that market to a wide range of people rank ease of pronunciation high on their list of criteria. That's for good reason. If you aren't confident you know how to say something, you are less likely to say it—and less likely to buy it. It doesn't matter if you're ordering a beer, asking for a pair of jeans, or requesting a book by an author with a difficult name. No one wants to look stupid.

So we hesitate. And that moment of hesitation can be a killer for companies.

Usually.

Nike is a huge success story. We could spend this whole book outlining that story. At the heart of it is an interesting name: Nike, the goddess of victory. Great meaning. Great imagery. But how do you say it again? In English, the word "Nike" would typically rhyme with the name "Mike." However, in Greek, that final e is long. "Nike" should rhyme with "Mikey." This is a significant disadvantage in English-speaking countries. But by putting out great products and associating themselves with celebrities, Nike has overcome this awkwardness.

Mixed Meaning

The desire for a unique name has spawned all sorts of new words, from Facebook to Spotify to Flickr. Sometimes they work great. Sometimes they are very awkward. And sometimes they are just sort of weird.

Microsoft is a good example of that last problem. Microprocessors are clearly important to the evolution of the personal computer. The same goes for software. Combine the first part of both words, and you get something that sounds pretty good. The o transitions nicely into the s, and the t at the end provides resolution. The name is gratifying to say. But on the surface, "microsoft" would seem to mean "small and cuddly." An unintentional weakness emerges from the initial good idea to merge the two words. Small and cuddly wouldn't be my first choice for an association when naming a global software behemoth. But, as you can see, they have overcome that weakness.

Confusing Combinations

Mergers are tough. There are competing interests. There is uncertainty. Who will still have jobs? Who will be made redundant? And what will we call the new entity? How do you signify a new direction with expanded capabilities while paying homage to the rich history of both organizations? Often you just smash the names together.

When I first heard the name Fifth Third Bank, I got excited. It was so weird. I assumed it was a reference to some hidden financial principle—like the fifth third is when profit is realized on an investment or something like that. (OK, math isn't my thing.) You can imagine my disappointment when I found out it was simply the result of a merger between Third National Bank and Fifth National Bank. A confounding name that hasn't stopped the bank from more than 100 years of success.

STEP 4 TAKEAWAYS ⟶

This was a big step. You built on the work you did in Steps 2 and 3 by using research to dramatically increase your list of potential names. You now have at least 30 more name options. Remember:

1. When conducting naming research, there are five good starting points: the thesaurus, an encyclopedia like Wikipedia, literature, insider lingo, and mythology.
2. It's OK to choose a word that you didn't previously know. Sometimes the best name is one you aren't familiar with.
3. You might need a reminder to relax at this point. It feels like there is a lot of pressure on you to make this decision. We looked at several examples of very successful companies that thrive even with challenging names.

DECIDING ON THE FINAL NAME

Great job. You have done some amazing work up to this point and created loads of possible names. Now it is time to eliminate some of the names on your list. This section will give you the tools you need to make these hard decisions. By the end of this step, you will cut your list down to ten possible finalists, and then emerge with the one name that is the best choice for you.

You made your list of criteria that you will use to judge possible names. You made brainstorming lists of words. You used those lists or words to come up with possible names. And you used research to expand your pool of names. Now it is time to narrow your focus. This is hard work. You will second-guess yourself. At different points, you will think all the names are good and all of them are terrible. That's how it goes.

Anyone who has named a company (or anything else, for that matter) has gone through this. I have doubts right up until I start giving the presentation to our clients. Even as I walk into the room, I'm thinking, "These are terrible! What am I doing?" But once I establish the context, lay out the criteria, and tell the story of the names, I remember all the hard work we put in, and I regain my confidence.

Trust the process. It has taken you this far. There's only one more step to get through, so let's go.

DECIDING WHAT TO CUT AND WHAT TO KEEP

At this point, you should have a list of about 50 names. They will generally fall into the categories from Step 3: real words, foreign language words, compound words, phrases, blended words, made-up words, and people and place names.

Within each of the categories, you might notice your names falling into subcategories. Let's say you have the words "bullhorn," "megaphone," and "microphone" in your list of real words. Once you group your possible names, you can easily eliminate the weaker ones. In this example, you might decide that "microphone" is too common, so it doesn't fit your unusualness criteria. Plus, a microphone relies on a speaker system to be amplified. That doesn't work metaphorically for what you want to do—you want something that can be heard on its own.

Meanwhile, "bullhorn" and "megaphone" are synonyms. They both amplify sound. They are self-contained. They are a similar length. You decide that the *l*, *h*, and *r* combination in "bullhorn" is a little hard to pronounce, so you choose "megaphone." But after researching your competition, you discover a direct competitor called Megaphone Marketing. So you decide you can live with *Bullhorn*.

The above example demonstrates the difficult process in Step 5: Make necessary decisions and decide what compromises you can live with. Your first choice will often have been taken by someone else. That's how it goes. Remember, that doesn't mean you've failed. Because you have gone through this naming process, *all* your shortlisted names will be better than 90 percent of the business names in the world. Most people don't think about these things when they name their businesses. You have.

There are no hard-and-fast rules for picking the best name. There are some time-honored guideposts, though. The following suggestions come from an essay published in the 1960s called "How to Launch a New Product." The advice on how to pick a name still holds true today:

+ Name should be simple, pronounceable, short, easy to write, and generally avoid bad associations.
+ Name should be legible in any size of font.
+ Name should sound harmonious and clear and be easily remembered and pronounceable in several languages.
+ Name should be original to avoid confusion with other products.

While this advice is more than 60 years old now, it is still useful. You want a name that sounds good and that is simple, legible, and original. No problem. With these factors in the back of your mind, you are now going to combine all the names you have generated so far into one master list. As you make your list, you can put a star next to the ones that meet this criteria. But don't go too crazy. We are still going to revisit your criteria list from Step 1.

Gathering Exercise

Go back through all the exercises in Steps 3 and 4. Write the words listed there in the space below. The rest of Step 5 will walk you through the process to narrow this list from 50 to fewer than 10. Refer back to this list as you read and start crossing them out as you work through the following sections.

_____

_____

_____

_____

_____

_____

_____

_____

_____

_____

_____

_____

_____

_____

_____

_____

_____

_____

_____

_____

_____

_____

_____

_____

_____

_____

_____

_____

_____

_____

_____

_____

_____

_____

_____

_____

_____

CRITERIA

First, grab your criteria list from the end of Step 1. Use those criteria to eliminate any words that don't meet your standards. Be ruthless. You will inevitably fall in love with a name, discover a valid reason to get rid of it, but justify keeping it through some complicated logic only you can comprehend. Don't fall in love. Hold out for a name that works within your criteria.

Good names aren't like Hollywood romances. You don't usually fall in love at first sight. They grow on you. Great names are only great in retrospect. At the moment of decision, they feel risky. Your criteria will help you mitigate that risk. Below are some additional thoughts on criteria you might consider applying to your list.

Specificity

In a letter of advice to his brother, playwright Anton Chekhov famously said, "In descriptions of Nature one must seize on small details . . . you'll have a moonlit night if you write that on the mill dam a piece of glass from a broken bottle glittered like a bright little star." While it's unquestionably good advice for aspiring writers, it is also good advice for namers. Avoid the sea of undifferentiated names by getting specific.

Once you group your words into like types, eliminate the generic words in favor of the specific ones. A specific name will pique people's interest. A generic word will not. For example, you would eliminate the words "boat" and "rowboat" in favor of the more specific "oarlock." In my design agency example, I had "winter cap," the more specific "balaclava," and "gabardine," a material used to make winter caps. I would start by eliminating "winter cap" but keeping "balaclava," because it's so nice to say. But then it occurs to me that it might get confused with "baklava," and I don't want anyone to think my company is a pastry. So "gabardine" wins instead. Generally, specificity rules the day.

Overly Common Words

Your lists will have some words that are specific but still too common to be a good name. They likely have something to do with your industry. Get rid of them. In my design agency example, I would eliminate words like "design" and "logo" because they are generic and clichés in my industry.

The counterargument is Apple (which seems to be a counter-argument for a lot of naming conventions). That is an awfully common word. But it doesn't have anything to do with computers, so it works. I mentioned the word "tinfoil" in Step 4. Even though it is common, it might make the cut because it is out of context for a design agency.

Also remember that the company you know as Apple today was once called Apple Computer Inc. until it was large enough to drop the "Computer" from its name. So you can choose a common word for your name, but you might need a modifier to help pave the way for your brand until your keyword can stand on its own. You may love the word "stove," but you will have to be known as Stove Denim until your jeans can compete with Levi's.

Spelling

This is likely already in your criteria. But if it isn't, it can still be a useful tool to decide between similar words. Say one of your passions is dinosaurs. That works out great because you are starting a company that specializes in rare books. On your list, perhaps you have two favorite words: "brontosaurus" and "quetzalcoatlus." You can safely eliminate "quetzalcoatlus" as exceedingly difficult to spell and tedious to type. Plus, Brontosaurus Books sounds great.

You might like the name Apple, but you don't want to get sued by one of the largest brands in the world, so you translate it. Is Manzana or Pomme easier to spell? What about Seb or Apfel? You can probably safely discard Pingguo. Even though it is longer, the short, easy syllables of Manzana might make for the best name.

The Toddler Test

You also might have pronunciation in your criteria. Use it now, either way. I mentioned above eliminating "bullhorn" in favor of "megaphone" because the latter was easier to say. Some combinations of letters tend to be more difficult to pronounce. Think of what toddlers have a hard time saying: *j, l, r, s, sh, ch, th*. My wife, Laura, loves kids, but they just can't say her name. She gets Wowa, Lola, Lowa, and some combinations I can't figure out how to spell. To test a name's pronounceability, ask yourself, "Would a three-year-old have a hard time saying this?"

Also note that if your company intends to do business internationally, pronunciation is a major consideration. For example, native Japanese speakers have troubles with some combinations that are easy for people who speak a Slavic language. There are even regional differences. A Spanish speaker from Spain might have no problem with the *th* combination, while a Spanish speaker from Mexico would likely find it very difficult. Research the regions in which you intend to do business, and ask native speakers which words and sounds are difficult to say. While you are at it, make sure (if it is an English word) that it doesn't mean something terrible in those languages.

Looks

This might sound crazy, but some words look better than others. I think Marlboro is a beautiful word. The combination of letters that ascend above the midline creates a nice visual cadence; up, down, up, down. In fact, Bullhorn has a similar visual cadence. Capitalizing the first letter of each word is called title case. Type your words out in title case. Which looks more interesting? Which do you find more pleasing: Wahoo, Yahoo, or Yoo-hoo?

Visual cadence also has a practical side. We can recognize words by their shape before we can read the individual letters. That is why highway signs are always in title case and never in all caps. We can recognize the shapes traveling 70 miles per hour before we can read the words. "Tulsa" is easier to recognize than "TULSA."

However, you should also try writing your name in all caps. Capital letters are good at commanding attention. A name in all caps forces the reader to pause because the blocky shape is more difficult to read. Signs that say things like DO NOT ENTER are written in all caps. Same with important ones like STOP. Before you eliminate a word because it doesn't look nice in title case, try putting it in all caps. It might work well—and it might make sense for your company strategically.

Short List Exercise

From all your scribbling in the space above, locate the ten names that made the cut. Write the remaining names here:

1. _____

2. _____

3. _____

4. _____

5. _____

6. _____

7. _____

8. _____

9. _____

10. _____

HOW TO TEST YOUR IDEA

When beta testing your name, my first inclination is to say "Don't." Be confident. Stick to your choice. But that's hard to do. This is a big decision, and you have probably lost some perspective on it as you have worked through this process. You have likely never named a company before and will want some assurance that you aren't totally crazy. Most people will at least want to run a couple of names by their friends to check their thinking. That is a good impulse. You are putting a lot of effort into this and don't want to mess it up. I get it.

But some ways of getting feedback are better than others. Remember, everyone has an opinion, and most of them aren't informed. They also lack your vision of the future. The people you are crowdsourcing haven't gone through this name-generation process or taken the time to picture the name in context. Their reactions can be useful, though. Here is how to set up a test for your list of name finalists.

Create a Deck

Using the presentation software of your choice, find a photo that is relevant to your industry. Place the image in the background of the slide and make it darker so the word will be legible in white text. Create two slides for each name using two different fonts. For the first slide, use Helvetica. For the second, use Times New Roman. It is a good idea to use a background image. The image will make it feel more like a brand name and less like a word on a screen or piece of paper. I would use the same image on each slide to ensure your group is responding to the word and not the image.

Your name will never again show up on a blank piece of paper, so if you present it that way, you are doing yourself a disservice. People must be able to imagine the name as something that stands for a company, not just a word on paper.

Run a Focus Group

Gather a small focus group. The best group will have a broad cross-section of people. Ideally, they would be potential customers, but that might be logistically difficult. The main thing you want to ensure is that you have a range of people, from those who know a lot about language to those who have a fairly low literacy level. By that I mean people who don't read much or think critically about language. (This will be easy because that is the majority of people.) This kind of group will give you valuable insight into how very different people will respond to your potential names. One person's "I love it!" is someone else's "No way. I don't get it."

Give your focus group 30 seconds with each slide, or a total of 60 seconds per name. Have them rate it from 1 to 10. Also ask them to jot down a few initial impressions. Then go back through and tell them a few sentences giving the back story to each name. Have them note down if knowing what the name means makes their reaction more or less favorable. This will tell you if an origin story will help the name or hurt it.

Tally up the results. This information shouldn't make the decision for you, but it will tell you how some people might respond to your name. Here is a word of caution from Alexandra Watkins in her book *Hello, My Name Is Awesome*: "Because language belongs to all of us, most people feel very qualified to comment on it. What's tricky is that we are not very good at drawing the line as to which bits of linguistic comment require specialist knowledge and which don't."[1] In other words, listen to what people say about the name, but remember that they are not experts. Often people feel obligated to give their opinion when asked, even if they have no knowledge base for making that judgment.

HOW TO PICK JUST ONE

After eliminating some names with the above criteria and testing the remaining names with your focus group, you should now have fewer than five names on your list. Here are a couple of concrete ways to narrow your list down even more and determine which name is the best choice for you.

State Business Name Search

Go to your secretary of state's website to see if the name is already registered in your state. There is likely to be some competition for many names. You have to be able to register your name with the state to do business there, so the level of competition will help you eliminate some of your choices. Making sure no other business has your exact name is important; however, you will likely find names that are similar or that use some parts of your proposed name. For example, you might find an Acme Business Solutions. That does not prohibit you from registering Acme Pools as a business name.

At this point, you aren't actually registering any names. You are simply using the state business name search tool to whittle down your shortlist of names. You will likely be able to eliminate one or more names because they are too similar to another name in your state and in your industry.

Basic Market Research

Next, do some Google searches to check for direct competitors with the same or similar names. Try looking by geography. For example, if you wanted to start an athletic shoe company in the Pacific Northwest called Nike (obviously not a good idea), you could search for "Nike Portland." Or you can search by type of business: "Nike Athletic Shoes." Or "Nike running shoes."

You can do similar searches on social media platforms. Sometimes international companies will show up there that you might have missed elsewhere. Again, this isn't a definitive approach to picking one name. These simple steps will eliminate any obvious, glaring issues that might come up, such as another company by the same or similar name in the same or a related industry. You won't catch everything with these searches, but don't worry—the next step will get anything you missed.

Trademarking

The next step is to run your finalists through a trademark search. You need to know if there is someone out there who already has and will defend the name you want to use. The easiest place to do this is at the U.S. Patent and Trademark Office's (USPTO) website (https://www.uspto.gov/). This isn't a substitute for applying for your own trademark (which we'll discuss in the next chapter). You are just trying to eliminate names that are already trademarked by someone else.

In the end, it comes down to a difficult decision. With all the criteria, care, and technique in the world, you still can't predict whether your customers will get it, love it, or just ignore it. You can put your best foot forward, though. And this process is oriented toward that goal.

As we mentioned earlier, taking a little time to see which name grows on you is a good idea. It is common to fall in and out of love with names in the first couple of days. But taking too long is just delaying the decision. You shouldn't need to sit with your shortlist for more than a week or so. Make your choice and get to work.

Congratulations! If you have made it this far, you have your name. You trusted the process and put in the necessary work. That is no small feat.

CASE STUDY
SONOS

This is a good case study for you to think about as you move on to the next steps. You have named your company, and now you need to transition into the design process. This case study looks at how meaning sometimes sits on the border between language and design.

Some words just feel right. "Sonos" is one of those words. It isn't English or foreign, but it isn't exactly made up, either. The root is the Latin word sono (to make sound), which is also the root for words like "sound" and "sonnet." It goes deeper than that, though. Sono is descended from swen, meaning to make sound, from the older Proto-Indo-European language spoken more than 4,000 years ago. Humans have been familiar with this language construction for a long time. And it persists to the current era:

+ Spanish: sonar (to make a sound)

+ French: sonner (to ring or sound)

+ Italian: suonare (to play an instrument)

Sonos feels foreign and familiar at the same time. This is a great strategy for the startup. They want people to have an idea of what they do: that it relates to sound. But the name doesn't carry the potential baggage of other real words.

Another unusual element is that the name is a palindrome (it reads the same backward and forward). This is emphasized by the company's design choices. First, the word is displayed in all capital letters. This has two effects. One, as I have mentioned, all caps is harder to read, so you have to pay more attention. This might be a bad thing for highway signs, but it can be good for a company that wants you to stop and look at the name. The second is that the s at the beginning and the one at the end are the same size: SONOS looks and feels different from Sonos.

CASE STUDY, CONT.

In addition, the designer chose a sans serif font, emphasizing the reflexive visual. The capital *N* reads the same forward and backward. A serif font wouldn't have that effect. The way the word looks reiterates the idea of "sound." The word looks like surround sound feels. It looks like an echo, like reverberations. The word looks like it is wearing headphones.

The way the word itself sounds is important, too. "Sonos" is easy to say. It sounds liquid, like the sound of wind in the trees. It is soothing; it is smooth. The company sells a system that makes listening to music easier. And they want to sell it to as many people as possible; it isn't a high-end, $100,000 system. The name of the company shouldn't sound complex or elitist. It should sound intuitive—and it does. The sound of the word reflects and reiterates the brand's value proposition.

Sonos is a great name for a startup company selling a better way to listen to your media. It is also a good note to leave you on. This name bridges the language exercises we have been discussing with the design decisions facing you next. The designer here made four choices that reiterate the effect of the name:

+ There is no logo to get in the way.

+ The name is set in all caps.

+ The name is set in a sans serif typeface with a middle N that reads the same both ways.

+ Finally, the designer often repeats the name to emphasize the echo effect.

Design affects how the name looks. And how a name looks can either emphasize or de-emphasize potential connotations. Keep that in mind as you read through the next chapter.

STEP 5 TAKEAWAYS ——▶

The bulk of Step 5 helped you go from a list of words to a shortlist of names to a final name choice. We revisited the criteria you developed in Step 1 and used additional criteria to shorten the list. Once the list was down to a short handful of finalists, you read about how to test those names with small focus groups. You also read about how to begin the process of checking name availability.

1. When deciding between words, use more specific words over more general ones, avoid common words unless they are out of context, and remember that spelling and pronunciation are essential criteria.

2. The look of a word matters. We talked about the shape of the word "Marlboro" as an example and discussed how typography can affect the look of a word. Use this as a final consideration when making the hard decisions.

3. There are three methods to begin the search for name availability: Checking your secretary of state's website, searching through Google or other search engines, and searching with the USPTO.

LIFE AFTER
CHOOSING A NAME

This has been a lot of work, and hopefully you have learned about how to brainstorm and choose a name for your brand. But while we are at the end of the naming journey, your new venture is just beginning. This chapter is primarily about how to use the name as part of your business strategy and what other pieces of language you might need. As we mentioned in the introduction, the name is the tip of the iceberg. The first priority is how to secure the iceberg, but we also need to start discussing how to build out everything under the water.

There are some things about your brand you aren't going to be able to control. It is primarily composed of other people's perceptions, based on their experiences. If you don't take the time to say who you are, someone else will decide for you, and you may not like what you hear. This chapter contains three exercises that will help you lay the foundations, to give your intentions for the brand the best chance of shining through.

But first, let's take a step back. Some people will have made it to the end of the naming process I've laid out here without settling on a name. Don't despair. You have the tools and resources you need to get through this.

WHAT IF YOU STILL DON'T HAVE A NAME?

There is a chance that this book left you discouraged, confused, and without a name. I am sure that is because the naming process can be complex, not because the book lacked clarity or effectiveness. Right?

Luckily, you have a few options at this point. You likely know someone with a knack for language. You can hire them to go through this book and generate a new set of words for you to analyze. You can con a spouse or a friend into helping you. You can probably find a verbose college student who would be thrilled to do it for pizza and beer.

I have a friend who was working through an early version of this book. She was starting a company to help teachers with continuing education and best practices. She had been thinking about it so long that she was stuck on a couple of names that were clichés in her industry. She couldn't shake them even after doing a couple of the exercises, so she asked her husband to try.

By combining their lists, they found a name they both loved. Was it because he was better at naming? Absolutely not. He simply thinks very literally. That meant he could provide grounding language to counter her more abstract language. Together, they clicked.

It might be that your situation is particularly complex, not that you are struggling with the naming process. That is why people hire agencies like Bullhorn. If you are in a highly competitive international market, you probably need some professional help.

Maybe you have narrowed the list to a handful of options. You showed the names to your friends, and they muddied the waters and created some self-doubt. Your spouse hates them all. Your parents think you are crazy. You want to go back to the job you hated just so you don't have to think about it for another second. Send us that list. We will provide clear feedback that helps you make a decision, feel good about it, and stick with it. You have resources at your disposal. Do not despair.

FORMALIZING YOUR NAME

But on the other end of the naming spectrum lies success. Let's say you have chosen your name. You have your big idea. What is the next step? How do you formalize your name so you can start to work? First, you will need to register your name with the state in which you will do business. You already did a quick business name and trademark search in Step 5. Now you need to go back and register it. But first, let's clarify some vocabulary before moving on. Fair warning: What follows wades into some legal lingo. I am not a lawyer. This should be taken as general information and guideposts, not legal advice. I recommend seeking the guidance of a lawyer throughout the process.

Copyright or Trademark

These function similarly, in the sense that they both protect your intellectual property. They work a little differently, though. You will likely generate copyrightable material through the course of your business. If you write a book or a blog post, create a course, or design an image, those things can all be copyrighted. But your business name (or the title of your book, for that matter) cannot be.

For protection of business names, we must look to trademarks. The USPTO defines a trademark in this way: "A trademark is a brand name. A trademark or service mark includes any word, name, symbol, device, or any combination, used or intended to be used to identify and distinguish the goods/services of one seller or provider from those of others, and to indicate the source of the goods/services." That gets us to the next distinction.

Trademark or Service Mark

The details here are a little in the weeds, but they might be important to you. A *trademark* protects companies selling a product. Nike and Budweiser are trademarks. A *service mark* protects a company providing a service. The store where you buy your Nike shoes or the bar where you buy your Budweiser beer will likely have a service mark. They are providing you the *service* of selling you the product.

You have undoubtedly seen organizations use the ® symbol after their brand name. That is for use once the USPTO has officially registered your trademark or service mark. While you are waiting for their approval, you can use ™ or ℠ to indicate that you intend to register.

To Trademark or Not to Trademark

That is the question. If you decide to trademark, you are obligated to defend it. That will cost you time and money (most often by hiring a lawyer). And yes, that time and money will be well-spent. There are famous cases of companies failing to enforce their trademarks and losing them. Here are a few examples:

+ *Escalator*: Originally trademarked by the Otis Elevator Co. in 1900; lost in 1950.
+ *Yo-yo*: Trademarked in 1932; 33 years later a court ruled the trademark had been improperly registered.
+ *Zipper*: Registered in 1925; five years later people were using the word so widely it had become a generic term, and the company lost the trademark.

In general, it is a good idea to pursue a trademark. There are some competitive markets where trademarking is absolutely essential. If you know you want to trademark, or think you might, consult a trademark attorney.

You can also submit the name for trademark approval online. In order for the name to be registrable, the USPTO is looking for two things. One, the mark has to be unique. It can't be spelled or pronounced the same as another registered trademark. If it is similar to other trademarks, they go to the next criterion: Is the similarly named company selling related goods or services?

"Related" doesn't necessarily mean exactly the same. A consumer often buys milk and yogurt from the same company, for example. So if your company makes yogurt, a milk manufacturer with a similar name would be considered related.

The USPTO offers some guidance on what qualities make for a strong name that is more likely to be accepted. It has four categories to consider.

The first two are unregistrable:

1. *Generic*. This would be like starting a bicycle company and trying to register the brand name Bicycle.
2. *Descriptive*. This would be trying to register a name that explicitly describes the product, like Lightweight Bicycles.

The third and fourth categories are stronger and can be registered:

3. *Suggestive*. This is similar to our earlier discussion of metaphors. If you wanted to suggest lightweight bikes, you might try to register the name Feather Bicycles.
4. *Fanciful/Arbitrary*. The PTO considers this to be the strongest category. Names here would be from the made-up or blended categories; they are new words or words that are totally out of context. Denim Bicycles might be a valid trademark because while "denim" is a common word, it is out of context, or arbitrary, for a bicycle company.

BUILDING YOUR FOUNDATIONAL LANGUAGE

Once you have that final name and have taken care of any legal concerns, you can move on to developing some foundational language to accompany it as part of your brand naming package. This will set you apart from most other businesses. This language is the foundation of all other writing about the brand: headlines, descriptions, biographies. The three primary items of this core foundation language are the tag line, elevator pitch, and values. They all derive from your name, and all play an integral role in building your brand recognition.

Descriptive Tag Line

Not every business needs a tag line. If you chose a descriptive name, you can skip this. But if you picked a less literal name, it is probably a good idea to have a tag line as a transitional piece of language until your name is recognizable. The descriptive tag line is not like Nike's "Just Do It." That is sometimes called a tag line, but it is really more of a mantra for the organization. You need a descriptive tag line that tells people what you do. Here are a few tips and guideposts for how to write this line:

1. Think of the descriptive tag line as a book's subtitle. The title is compelling, while the subtitle tells you exactly what to expect: Five Steps to Creating Brand and Product Names That Sell.
2. Try to restrict yourself to five words or less. This forced brevity will make you get to the point as quickly as possible.
3. Don't repeat words. Due to the small amount of space you have to work with, don't reuse anything from your name.
4. If you are stuck, try doing the next two exercises first and then come back to this one. They might give you some ideas.

As you think about your tag line, try to be as specific as possible without excluding parts of your business. "Commercial Electrical Contractors" wouldn't be a good tag line if you also do residential or industrial work. Conversely, "General Contracting" is probably too broad if you focus on electrical work. Look at your tag line and ask yourself two questions: Is it too specific? Is it too general? The answer to both should be no.

Descriptive Tag Line Exercise

Based on the above guideposts, write five potential descriptive tag lines for your business. After you finish, scratch out the three weakest. What is left? Sit with the two remaining for a couple of days. Keep the one that feels the most natural to say.

1. _____

2. _____

3. _____

4. _____

5. _____

Elevator Pitch

You may already have an elevator pitch: a quick, 30-second-long summary of what your business does. Work through this exercise anyway. It will help clarify your thinking. A good elevator pitch contains three elements: what you do, how you do it, and why. Let's unpack these:

1. *What*? What product or service do you offer, in the plainest language possible?
   Example: Bullhorn is a branding agency.

2. *How*? What do you do differently from everyone else? Is it your process, your proprietary technology?
   Example: We build confident brands with language and design.

3. *Why*? This is important. This is the part that should resonate with your potential customers and future co-workers. You could do anything. Why did you decide to do this? What do you care about?
   Example: Our purpose is to help mission-driven brands succeed.

From these three pieces, you will write your elevator pitch. It could be as simple as stringing these three sentences together, or you can wordsmith them to death. It really doesn't matter if you ever say it out loud. Going through this exercise will give you clarity about what sort of company you are building.

Elevator Pitch Exercise

Based on the example above, write your What, How, and Why. Write two variations for each.

What?

1. _____

2. _____

How?

1. _____

2. _____

Why?

1. _____

2. _____

Now take the pieces you have written and write a concise paragraph explaining to someone what you do, how you are unique, and why they should care.

_____

_____

_____

_____

_____

_____

_____

_____

_____

_____

Values

The next element of foundational language is your values. How you articulate your values is what makes you unique. You can even use sticky notes for this exercise, so you feel like you are doing real creative work. I am joking, but only partly. The sticky notes actually help. Here is a three-step process to help you figure out your fundamental values. You will think about your values through three different lenses and then assess them as a set.

1. Get five sticky notes and write a word that describes you on each note. Don't just use any descriptor—choose five things that are especially true in light of this venture. What parts of yourself can you bring to the work? It could be anything: creativity, fun, hard work, rigor, decisiveness, etc.

2. Get five more notes. This time, think about your ideal employee. What are five words you would use to describe them? Are they diligent or silly? Are they world-class or kind? There's no right or wrong answers, but it sometimes helps your language get

more precise if you can picture a real person. Who would you love to hire? Who is your current star employee?

3. Again, choose five new sticky notes. This time, ask yourself what language an outsider would use when describing you or your organization. Would they say your company is cutting-edge, service oriented, or both? It would be best if you picture an actual customer. The five words will be more precise. If not, who else knows what you are doing? What might they say?

Once you have finished the three perspectives, put all 15 sticky notes on the wall. The first ones you are going to remove are the aspirational values. Those are the things you hope will be true someday, but aren't yet true today. There is space for those values, but it's not here. Here they would be disingenuous.

Next we are going to take a cue from business consultant Patrick Lencioni. He often talks about "permission to play" values. These are values that are true of just about anyone running a sustainable business—things like integrity and being truthful. They are the basic minimum standards for being in business. They would only count as values for your business if you adhered to them in some extreme, over-the-top way. And in business, "extreme" tends to cost you money. So now get rid of all the "permission to play" values.

Now organize whatever is left. Start by combining similar concepts into columns—sometimes called affinity mapping. You want to end up with between three and seven columns. Those are your values. Pick the word or phrase that best represents that column. That will leave you with three to seven values. It would also be helpful to write something longer to give the values context.

These remaining values are the core of your language. They are who you are even if you change the elevator pitch. Your values don't change unless you hire people who change the company's culture. You can use these to formulate questions for hiring and to assess employees you have to fire. They can help you choose your office building, your type of sign, or your uniforms.

I suggest you post them publicly. We do this at Bullhorn. Here is a short version of our values:

+ Empathy + Honesty
+ Dissatisfaction + Improvement
+ Creativity + Decisiveness

Here are two more examples of company values that are quite different, but still very effective:

The Container Store

1. Great Person = 3 Good People
2. Communication IS Leadership
3. Fill the other guy's basket to the brim. Making money then becomes an easy proposition.
4. The Best Selection, Service & Price
5. Intuition does not come to an unprepared mind. You need to train before it happens.
6. Man in the desert selling.
7. Air of excitement

Zappos

1. Deliver WOW Through Service
2. Embrace and Drive Change
3. Create Fun and a Little Weirdness
4. Be Adventurous, Creative, and Open-Minded
5. Pursue Growth and Learning
6. Build Open and Honest Relationships with Communication
7. Build a Positive Team and Family Spirit
8. Do More with Less
9. Be Passionate and Determined
10. Be Humble

Values Exercise

If you don't want to play with sticky notes, we've given you room to do the exercise here. Make your three categories of five words. Eliminate what isn't central, and combine similar ideas:

You:

1. _____

2. _____

3. _____

4. _____

5. _____

Co-worker:

1. _____

2. _____

3. _____

4. _____

5. _____

Outsider:

1. _____

2. _____

3. _____

4. _____

5. _____

Your Values:

1. _____

2. _____

3. _____

4. _____

5. _____

6. _____

7. _____

8. _____

9. _____

10. _____

HOW DO I GO FROM A NAME TO A LOGO?

The inevitable next question is graphic design. You have your name, and you want the design to be as thoughtful as the naming process. There are a few ways to go, depending on your budget and timeline. The good news is that all the time you have spent thinking about your brand will help the designers in their work. Bring all the assets you have created in this chapter to the introductory design meeting. This will save you time and money.

Online Logo Generator

You didn't use an online name generator, although there are several (I personally love the Wu-Tang Names Generator). You want your name to represent you and your intentions. The same goes for design. Online logo generators create exactly what you would expect: the most obvious, common idea, poorly executed. The price is compelling, but with design, you really do get what you pay for. I am not going to suggest any here because they go in and out of business quickly. But a search for online logo design will give you a few bad options.

Freelance Designer

There is a wide range of freelancers, from your friend's cousin in high school who is artsy (don't hire them) to the freelancer who does design work for huge companies like Nike and Google. There are some things about working with a freelancer that you might really like or hate. For one, you work directly with the designer. If the relationship is healthy, this can be extremely rewarding. If the relationship isn't great, it can be genuinely terrible. You also aren't paying for support you might not need at this point. Freelancers generally have fairly low overhead, and their pricing tends to reflect that.

The good thing about hiring a freelance designer is that they will have previous work online. Any serious designer will have a portfolio website. If you want to meet the designer in person, start with a search of logo designers in your area. But there is no reason you should restrict yourself. There are a few sites where you can see work from designers all over the world:

+ Dribbble (https://dribbble.com/)
+ Behance (https://www.behance.net/)
+ Working Not Working (https://workingnotworking.com/)

Design Agency

There are also many types of design agencies, from global firms that can help you launch your product internationally to local agencies better suited to making ads for car dealerships. The advantage of an agency is the support it can offer you. Product managers keep the project on track, buffer you from the design team, and listen to you when you have panic attacks. Agencies also generally have a wider talent range: writers, digital strategists, designers, developers, etc. You will eventually need more than just a logo. You will need sales support tools, like a website and print materials. You will need photographs. Developing a strong relationship with an agency can help position you for years of success. Of course, it will be a little more expensive upfront.

Finding the right fit can be a challenge. There are design agencies in every city across the globe, and they all tend to have slick websites and talk a good game. You can't fake the work, though. Start by reading some design blogs. These blogs are lists of the best work curated by designers. You may not know design-related tidbits like the difference between kerning and leading, but these people will. They also link to the creators of the work. Find some work you like, and read about the agency that created it. If the design and language speak to you, reach out to them. Here are several reliable industry blogs:

+ Brand New (https://www.underconsideration.com/brandnew/)
+ Identity Designed (https://identitydesigned.com/)
+ Dieline (https://thedieline.com/)
+ Creative Review (https://www.creativereview.co.uk/)
+ Abduzeedo (https://abduzeedo.com/)
+ BP&O (https://bpando.org/)
+ It's Nice That (https://www.itsnicethat.com/)
+ Logo Design Love (https://www.logodesignlove.com/)
+ AIGA Eye on Design (https://eyeondesign.aiga.org/)

MY FAVORITE NAME

Whenever I talk about the topic of naming, the first question that always comes up is: "So what's your favorite name?" If you have made it this far, you can probably guess that I find it hard to answer. I could tell them that I like names that are effective, but I sometimes find those names aesthetically displeasing. But that isn't a very satisfying answer. People want to hear why Patagonia, Prada, or Prana is a great name. They want to learn about a cool linguistic trick or a hidden meaning.

I could talk about how complicated it is to name a brand, saying, "Well, I think of the name as a reference point for the brand ecosystem." Here's a good phrase I came across while researching for a naming project: *nictitating membrane*. It's a third eyelid some animals have that protects or moistens their eyes while they're still open. Look it up. You will be able to visualize what a person looks like when you insert the phrase "brand ecosystem" into a conversation.

To spare them (and me), I sometimes just tell them what I actually like, although that's hard for me to do. I would never do that in a formal presentation, because what I like doesn't matter. Our clients are paying for a name that will be effective. But at a cocktail party, maybe what I like does matter. Maybe it matters here, too. I have said a lot in this book about what is effective. I'm going to wrap this up by telling a quick story about what I like. Who knows? It might affirm your decision about your name.

When my son George (whom I mentioned at the beginning of this book) was 5 years old, he got into making beaded necklaces and bracelets. We had plastic tubs of beads and balls of stretchy cord all over the place. At first we thought he might make a few Christmas presents. (Grandparents are hard to buy for.) But he quickly let us know we were thinking too small.

A friend of ours ran an outdoor market once a month with vendors, food, and music. They held a special holiday market for last-minute shoppers, and George wanted to have a booth selling bracelets. Like many budding business magnates before him, he put his family to work. He got his brother into it. He had my wife working on them, and eventually I got dragged into it, too. We were making bracelets first thing in the morning, before dinner, and after dinner. They were everywhere.

I don't think he had ever heard me talk about purpose-driven enterprises. He had never learned that having a mission is a way to motivate labor, but he intuited it. Immigration was a frequent topic on the news during this time, and he was learning about famous immigrants at school. At home, we were talking about how refugees had come to our community. He decided he was going to donate the profits from his booth to our local refugee resettlement agency. We were inspired and doubled our output.

Nevertheless, I was a somewhat reluctant bracelet maker. I liked it, but I didn't have the knack for it that the rest of the family did. But I was excited about a part of the venture where I could really contribute: the branding. One night I said, "George, I can help you decide what we should call this business." He replied, "No thanks. I already know what it is called." I gave him my fiercest pitch. I reminded him that I do this for a living. He reiterated that he didn't need my help.

I said, "Well, what are you going to call it?" He replied, "It is called George's Jewels, of course." I shook my head and laughed. My wife laughed. The boys looked at us, confused. And so at cocktail parties, or coffee meetings, or whenever someone asks me what my favorite name is, I always say, "George's Jewels."

At the beginning of the book I talked about all the different Georgetowns and how they can get confusing. Georgetown is a good example of tradition gone wrong. George started with tradition and made it right. Here are three reasons I love it.

Surprising

I like names that are strange and surprising. I mentioned the design agency Mother in Step 4. I love that name. It is so weird. There is a web development company called Jackson Fish Market. I love that, too. Does it work for them? I don't know, but I like it. I find it surprising and fun to say. I want to hire them because I think they would be fun to work with.

George's Jewels is a genuinely surprising name. For those of you who were never a middle school boy in the United States, the word "jewels" (or sometimes "family jewels") is a colloquial term for private parts. George didn't know that, which made it funnier. From the expressions of the people walking by the booth, it was funny to them, too.

Simple

In my analysis of Evol in Step 1, I mentioned that I didn't like the name but thought it was effective. I don't like it because I think it is trying too hard. I like names that seem effortless, like they were meant to be. FireWire is one of those names. There are so many things that could have gone wrong: it rhymes, it's a compound, and it describes the product. But it works perfectly.

George's Jewels is the same. George made jewelry. Of course that should be the name. It is perfectly descriptive. It isn't overly clever. It also has repeated *j* and *s* sounds. Each word has two syllables, giving the name a symmetry that makes it fun to say. Altogether, these qualities tie the words together to make them feel like a single, unified name.

Origin Story

I also like names that mean something—that begin to tell you the company's story. Take Patagonia. They were traveling in South America. They wanted to make clothing that stood up to the rigors of mountaineering and to create a company that would protect wild places. Patagonia is a start to a story. So is Apple. Microsoft is a cul-de-sac. There is no story in that name. It has been a terrifically successful company, but I don't like the name.

The best thing about George's Jewels is the story. At the market, I stood out in the aisle flagging people down. I would say, "Hey, you need to visit George's Jewels. That little guy started making bracelets so he could get them to you and donate the money to support refugees in our community." They were by far the junkiest things I have ever sold. They were also the easiest sale I have ever made. It's hard to say no to George.

We were at the booth for about three hours. He sold enough bracelets and necklaces that he could pay back his investors (us) and still deliver a check to the refugee nonprofit for $250. Not bad for a five-year-old.

So that's what I like. But as I have said repeatedly, that doesn't really matter. Now that you are an expert at naming, what do *you* like? You started out with not much more naming experience than George. Now you are a seasoned pro. Take the name you have worked so hard to create and build a great business. Businesses are the cornerstone of our society, and we need more thoughtful people to lead them. While I hope I like your name, I want to love your business. Thank you for investing time in choosing your name and for the investment you are making for all of us when you build a business that gives people opportunities and provides the products and services that change our lives. I have faith in you. You can do it.

SUCCESS?

If you used this book to name your organization, I would love to hear about it. Email me at brad@thenamingbook.com and tell me about the creative ways you used language to find the name that was perfect for you.

ENDNOTES

INTRODUCTION

[1] Edmond S. Meany, *Vancouver's Discovery of Puget Sound* (Portland, OR: Binfords & Mort, 1942).

[2] Chiranjeev Kohli and Douglas W. LaBahn, "Creating Effective Brand Names: A Study of the Naming Process," *Journal of Advertising Research* 37, no. 1 (January/February 1997).

STEP 1

[1] Tina M. Lowrey, L. J. Shrum, and Tony M. Dubitsky, "The Relation Between Brand-Name Linguistic Characteristics and Brand-Name Memory," *Journal of Advertising* 32, no. 3 (Autumn 2003): 7-17.

[2] Lowrey et al., "The Relation Between Brand-Name Linguistic Characteristics and Brand-Name Memory," 7-17.

3 Anthony B. Fallon, Kim Groves, and Gerald Tehan, "Phonological Similarity and Trace Degradation in the Serial Recall Task: When CAT Helps RAT, But Not MAN," *International Journal of Psychology* 34, no. 5/6 (October-December 1999): 301-307.

4 Georgije Lukatela, Stephen J. Frost, and Michael T. Turvey, "Phonological Priming by Masked Nonword Primes in the Lexical Decision Task," *Journal of Memory and Language* 39 (November 1998): 666-683.

5 Tomoyoshi Inoue, "Encoding Activities by Preschool Children Under Orienting Versus Learning Instructions: Are Onomatopoeias Associated with More Concrete Images?" *Japanese Psychological Research* 33, no. 1 (1991): 11-17.

6 Michael J. Cortese, "Revisiting Serial Position Effects in Reading," *Journal of Memory and Language* 39, no. 4 (November 1998): 652-665.

7 Edward F. McQuarrie and David Glen Mick, "Figures of Rhetoric in Advertising Language," *Journal of Consumer Research* 22, no. 4 (March 1996): 424-438.

8 Richard J. Harris and Noah J. Mosier, "Memory for Metaphors and Similes in Discourse," *Discourse Processes* 28, no. 3 (January 1999): 257-270.

9 Kevin Lane Keller, Susan E. Heckler, and Michael J. Houston, "The Effects of Brand Name Suggestiveness on Advertising Recall," *Journal of Marketing* 62, no. 1 (January 1998): 48-57.

10 George M. Zinkham and Claude R. Martin Jr., "New Brand Names and Inferential Beliefs: Some Insights on Naming New Products," *Journal of Business Research* 15, no. 2 (April 1987): 157–172

STEP 2

[1] Tom Kelley and David Kelley, *Creative Confidence: Unleashing the Creative Potential Within Us All* (New York: Crown Business, 2013).

STEP 3

[1] Christopher Johnson, "Awkwordplay: Just Because You Can Doesn't Mean You Should," The Name Inspector, 2009, http://www.thenameinspector.com/awkwordplay/.

[2] Frankel, Alex. *Wordcraft: The Art of Turning Little Words into Big Business* (New York: Crown Publishing Group, 2004).

STEP 5

[1] Alexandra Watkins, *Hello, My Name Is Awesome: How to Create Brand Names That Stick* (Oakland, CA: Berrett-Koehler Publishers, 2014).

RESOURCES

BOOKS ABOUT NAMING

Altman, Eli. *Don't Call It That*. San Francisco, CA: ExtraCurricular Press, 2014.

Frankel, Alex. *Wordcraft: The Art of Turning Little Words into Big Business*. New York: Crown Publishing Group, 2004.

Rivkin, Steve, and Fraser Sutherland. *The Making of a Name: The Inside Story of the Brands We Buy*. New York: Oxford University Press, 2004.

Taylor, Neil. *The Name of the Beast: The Process and Perils of Naming Products, Companies and Brands*. London: Marshall Cavendish Business, 2007.

Watkins, Alexandra. *Hello, My Name Is Awesome: How to Create Brand Names That Stick*. Oakland, CA: Berrett-Koehler Publishers, 2014.

BOOKS ABOUT THE CREATIVE PROCESS

Belsky, Scott. *Making Ideas Happen: Overcoming the Obstacles Between Vision and Reality.* New York: Portfolio, 2010.

Gilbert, Elizabeth. *Big Magic: Creative Living Beyond Fear.* New York: Riverhead Books, 2015.

Kelley, Tom, and David Kelley. *Creative Confidence: Unleashing the Creative Potential Within Us All.* New York: Crown Business, 2013.

Pressfield, Steven. *The War of Art: Break Through the Blocks and Win Your Inner Creative Battles.* New York: Rugged Land, 2002.

Tharp, Twyla. *The Creative Habit: Learn It and Use It for Life.* New York: Simon & Schuster, 2003.

USEFUL WEBSITES

The Name Inspector (http://www.thenameinspector.com/)
A source for background information on naming and analysis of names

OneLook Thesaurus (https://www.onelook.com/thesaurus)
A thesaurus that is better linked and provides stranger answers than most

Onym (https://onym.co/)
This site provides lots of naming resources. It is especially helpful when looking for lists of obscure words.

United States Patent and Trademark Office (https://uspto.gov)
The official website of the USPTO

GLOSSARY

acronym. An abbreviation formed from the first letter of other words, where the new word is pronounced as a new word; e.g., NASA.

blend. A name composed of two words combined into one by overlapping syllables: pin + interest = Pinterest.

brainstorm. A creative activity where you allow your brain to free associate, combining ideas that don't normally go together. An act of divergent thinking.

compound. A name composed of two words placed together: Facebook

copyright. Legally protected category of materials, such as books, photographs, and videos.

criteria. A list of standards you use to make strategic decisions.

divergent thinking. A process in which you are looking for multiple possible answers, rather than one right answer.

free association. An exercise in which you write down thoughts as they occur, even if they have no apparent connection to the original thought.

initialism. An abbreviation formed from the first letter of other words, where the new word is pronounced as a series of letters; e.g., FBI.

made up. A created name that isn't explicitly based on a real word in any language.

modifier. A word that qualifies another word. In a company name, the modifier often refers to the brand's vertical.

palindrome. A word that reads the same backward and forward; e.g., radar.

phrase. A name composed of a short phrase; e.g., Outdoor Voices.

service mark. A registered mark for a company that provides services to its customers, such as a retail store or a restaurant.

trademark. A legally registered symbol or word that represents a company or product.

ACKNOWLEDGMENTS

THIS BOOK EMERGED organically out of the desire to create better names, so it is hard to appropriately thank everyone who helped. But I am going to give it a shot. A good place to start is with my fellow writers at Bullhorn who challenged me while working on this project: Carrie Shirley and Kate Baughman. I have also had the benefit of working with several great editors. Doris Settles encouraged me to take the project from loose ideas to a workable outline. Laura Flowers waded into the deep waters, straightening out commas and sloppy thinking throughout. And Jen Dorsey helped me take a thin, spare thing and turn it into a real book.

I also want to thank the rest of the team at Bullhorn. First, to Chris Jackson and Adam Kuhn, who, like seers, know how a thing should look before it even exists. To Cat

Wentworth and Jenny Cobb, who read through painful early editions and gave invaluable feedback about how someone might actually use the book. To the encouragement I received from my partners, Will Coffman and Will Jones, and the grace extended by co-workers, a profound thank you. I truly believe our work is making the world better.

And finally to our great clients, who have shown so much trust and patience. You didn't know we were experimenting on you. Until now. Thank you.

ABOUT THE AUTHOR

BRAD FLOWERS started Bullhorn, an agency that builds confident brands with language and design, in 2008, when he realized he didn't want to teach and wasn't prepared to do much else. Brad leads naming and language generation at Bullhorn. He has a degree in English literature, two kids, and a wife who reminds him he isn't as smart as he thinks he is.

INDEX

CPSIA information can be obtained
at www.ICGtesting.com
Printed in the USA
JSHW010044040220
3989JS00004B/6